KU-373-763

DK EYEWITNESS TOP 10 TRAVEL GUIDES

LAS VEGAS

CONNIE EMERSON

DORLING KINDERSLEY

LONDON • NEW YORK • MUNICH
MELBOURNE • DELHI
WWW.DK.COM

Left **Bellagio** Center **The Forum Shops at Caesars** Right **The Venetian**

A DORLING KINDERSLEY BOOK

www.dk.com

Produced by
Blue Island Publishing, London

Reproduced by Colourscan, Singapore
Printed and bound in Italy by Graphicom

First published in Great Britain in 2002
by Dorling Kindersley Limited
80 Strand, London WC2R 0RL
A Penguin Company

A CIP catalogue record is available from
the British Library.

ISBN 0 7513 3825 7

Within each Top 10 list in this book,
no hierarchy of quality or popularity is
implied. All 10 are, in the editors' opinion,
of roughly equal merit.

Contents

Las Vegas Top 10

**The information in this
DK Eyewitness Top 10 Travel Guide is checked annually.**

Every effort has been made to ensure that this book is as up-to-date as possible at the time
of going to press. Some details, however, such as telephone numbers, opening hours,
prices, gallery hanging arrangements, and travel information are liable to change. The
publishers cannot accept responsibility for any consequences arising from the use of this
book, nor for any material on third party websites, and cannot guarantee that any website
address in this book will be a suitable source of travel information. We value the views and
suggestions of our readers very highly. Please write to:
Senior Publishing Manager, DK Eyewitness Travel Guides,
Dorling Kindersley, 80 Strand, London WC2R 0RL.

Left **Golden Nugget Casino** Center left **Jubilee** Center right **Wedding chapel** Right **Legacy Golf**

Left **Fremont Street Experience** Right **Grand Canyon**

 Following pages **Vegas Vic, Glitter Gulch**

LAS VEGAS
TOP 10

LAS VEGAS TOP 10

🔟 Las Vegas Highlights

The Entertainment Capital of the World offers just about everything: the world's largest hotels; the brightest stars in show business; shops and restaurants that rival any on earth. It's true, too, that the lights are brighter in Las Vegas. Yet you don't have to go far from the glamour and glitter to find the natural beauty of lakes and the desert as well.

The Strip
The neon artery of gambling pulses with excitement. Imaginatively themed resorts make it a street that never sleeps *(see pp8–9)*.

2 Hoover Dam
An engineering marvel, the dam not only tamed the raging Colorado River but also created the enormous Lake Mead, providing myriad aquatic pursuits, just minutes from the Las Vegas city limits *(see pp10–11)*.

3 Glitter Gulch
The heart of Las Vegas in its early days, downtown's centerpiece, Glitter Gulch, experienced a rebirth in the late 1990s *(see pp12–13)*.

4 Bellagio
The hotel that upped the ante as far as Las Vegas luxury is concerned. It is well located, too *(see pp14–15)*.

The Venetian 6
The Italian Renaissance revisited. Minstrels and nobility stroll among the Venetian landmarks; gondoliers glide by *(see pp20–21)*.

5 Grand Canyon
The ultimate excursion from Las Vegas. Whether their trip is by airplane, bus, or automobile, most visitors say the experience is unforgettable *(see pp16–19)*.

Aladdin 7
Visions of magic lamps and genies in bottles shimmer amid the hotel's minarets *(see pp22–3)*.

Red Rock Canyon 8
Not far from the city lights, this escarpment shimmers in the setting sun *(see pp24–5)*.

The Forum Shops at Caesars 9
The glory that was Rome provides the backdrop for the city's best upscale shops and restaurants *(see pp26–7)*.

Madame Tussaud's Wax Museum 10
Rub shoulders with the stars of the entertainment and sporting worlds, and learn how wax reproductions look so very real *(see pp28–9)*.

🔟 The Strip

Nowhere are the glitz and glitter of Las Vegas, or its ambivalence, so apparent as along the Strip. This 4-mile (6-km) long thoroughfare (actually a section of Las Vegas Boulevard) is the entertainment capital of the world and home to many of the largest hotels and casinos on the planet. The extravaganza of both its adult entertainment and family favorites makes Las Vegas a city of superlatives. The Strip is a master of reinvention, selling itself on seemingly contradictory values: hedonism one decade, family fun the next.

The Strip by day

🍩 You're on vacation – why *not* have doughnuts for breakfast?! Delicious "Krispy Kreme" doughnuts, current food fad of the western USA, are on sale at Excalibur, at the entrance to Treasure Island, and in other Strip casinos.

✪ To experience the excitement fully, get a hotel room with a view of the Strip. Best of all are the upper floors of the Venetian or Treasure Island, facing south.

Put on your shopping shoes early to beat the crowds at stores along the Strip. Or else patronize the hotel shops, which stay open until late.

• Map M3–R2 • General information: Las Vegas Convention and Visitors Bureau • 3150 Paradise Road • 702 892 0711 • www.lasvegas 24hours.com

Top 10 Sights

1. The Strip by Night
2. The Strip by Day
3. Older Hotel-Casinos
4. Theme Casinos
5. The Five Megaresorts
6. Fashion Show Mall
7. The Forum Shops at Caesars
8. Hole-in-the-Wall Businesses
9. Wet'n'Wild
10. Impersonators

1 The Strip by Night
After dark is when the Strip is meant to be seen: its miles of neon tubes, millions of twinkling, pulsing, flashing lights, vast fiber-optic signs, and, of course, thousands of people create an almost euphoric excitement.

2 The Strip by Day
Although daytime lacks the glitter of the night, the Strip starts coming to life from mid-morning, when the street and sidewalks become thronged with cars and pedestrians. The Strip is one of 15 American thoroughfares designated as an "All American Road and Scenic Byway."

3 Older Hotel-Casinos
Westward Ho, Riviera, Tropicana *(left)*, and Bally's are among the few surviving hotel-casinos of the 1950s to 1970s. Their façades and landscaping are grand but not over-the-top, reflecting the postwar era. Room prices are relatively low.

For more on the Strip See pp70–77

Theme Casinos
The MGM Grand, Treasure Island *(see p33)*, Monte Carlo, Luxor, and Caesars Palace *(see p32)* were all built in the early 1990s. As their names suggest, they are designed around themes. MGM Grand features a lion enclosure with real lions, Treasure Island *(right)* stages rousing pirate battles. Ancient Egypt is the theme of the Luxor.

6 Fashion Show Mall
Fashion Show Mall *(see p52)* is an upscale shopping center that is in the midst of an extensive renovation. When completed in 2003, the mall will be one of only three in the USA to have no fewer than eight major department stores as anchors.

7 The Forum Shops at Caesars
A Las Vegas must-see, the Forum Shops *(see pp26–7, above)* combine entertainment, dining, and shopping. Let your taste buds tingle on a burger while your eyes feast on scenes from ancient Rome.

5 The Five Megaresorts
Bellagio *(see pp14–15)*, Venetian *(pp20–21, right)*, Aladdin *(pp22–3)*, Mandalay Bay *(p32)*, and Paris *(p33)* have all opened since 1998. Once you are installed there is no need to venture out again: all your desires are catered for.

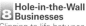

8 Hole-in-the-Wall Businesses
Clinging to life between the skyscrapers are simple one-story buildings that house everything from snack shops to tour operators. In one storefront operation men hand-roll cigars.

9 Wet 'n' Wild
Water heaven for kids and teenagers *(see p66)*. Experience thrill rides, a surf lagoon, and a "lazy river" for floating. Volleyball courts (dry) are thrown in for good measure.

10 Impersonators
Elvis lives – at least, his numerous reincarnations do. Elvis Presley and Marilyn Monroe impersonators, among others, are a routine sight on the Strip. They perform in nostalgia shows; some even perform marriage ceremonies. Keep your eyes open, though: some real celebrities live here too!

The Mob
As is vividly portrayed in the 1995 Robert de Niro movie *Casino*, organized crime and Las Vegas were natural bedfellows for several decades from the 1940s. Gangsters were drawn like magpies to the glittering coins piling up effortlessly in so many slot machines. Bugsy Siegel was the trailblazer with his Flamingo Hotel *(see p30)*, while Midwest crime boss Moe Dalitz opened the Desert Inn in 1950. These days, improved regulation and policing appear to have virtually eliminated Mob involvement.

🔟 Hoover Dam

Before the construction of the Hoover Dam early last century, the mighty Colorado River frequently flooded countless acres of farmland in southern California and Mexico. A series of studies into how to tame the rampaging river led in 1928 to the Boulder Canyon Project Act and the subsequent construction of the dam. This colossus of concrete – a triumph of engineering – not only provides flood control and generates electricity, but is also a huge tourist attraction, with nearly a million visitors a year.

The top of the dam

🥤 Before you leave Las Vegas, stock up on beverages and mouthwatering sandwiches at Capriotti's Sandwich Shop (324 W. Sahara) to have as a picnic later on a Lake Mead beach.

🚢 Take a cruise that does not include meals: it will be cheaper and give you more time to take in the surroundings.

Drive along the west shore of Lake Mead on highways 166 and 167, to access the Valley of Fire and Lost City Museum *(see p98).*

• Map T2 • 30 miles (50 km) SE of Las Vegas • Alan Bible Visitors Center, Hwy 93 at Lakeshore Rd • 702 293 8906 • Open 8:30am–4:30pm daily • Tour reservations 866 291 TOUR • Short tour $10, long tour $25 • www.hooverdam.com

Top 10 Sights

1. Hoover Dam Overlook
2. Alan Bible Visitors Center
3. Guided Tours
4. Lake Mead
5. Black Canyon River Raft Trips
6. Lake Mead Cruises
7. Scuba Diving
8. Boulder City/ Hoover Dam Museum
9. Construction Workers' Houses
10. Commercial District, Boulder City

Hoover Dam Overlook 1

For a lasting first impression, stop at the overlook on Highway 93 as you approach the dam from Las Vegas. The vista point is often crowded, but stop anyway: the sight of 3.2 million cu yards (2.6 million cu m) of concrete, standing 727 ft (221 m) high and erected by thousands of workers laboring around the clock for four years, is truly awe-inspiring.

Alan Bible Visitors Center 2

Audiovisual and theater presentations as well as multimedia exhibits explain the processes and perils involved in building this eighth wonder of the modern world. An overlook on top of the center provides an eagle-eye view of the dam, Lake Mead, and the Black Canyon.

Guided Tours 3

Take your pick of two tours (one short, one long) 525 ft (160 m) into the heart of the dam *(below).* The statistics of all that power are overwhelming.

For more on the Hoover Dam and Lake Mead **See pp92–7**

4 Lake Mead

The dam's lake is the largest man-made body of water in the USA. Its 550 miles (880 km) of shoreline boast forests, canyons, and flower-rich meadows; its waters abound with fish. Boulder Beach offers the best swimming.

6 Lake Mead Cruises

The lake's shores come to colorful life from the deck of a boat (left). You'll see sandy beaches and rocks of every hue. There's wildlife, too – look out for burros, jack rabbits, lizards, and the occasional bighorn sheep.

7 Scuba Diving

An unusual underwater scene greets divers: in addition to fish, there is a submerged factory where the dam's concrete was mixed, and the drowned community of St. Thomas. Take a trip with a local company; certified divers can scuba gear.

9 Construction Workers' Houses, Boulder City

Up to 8,000 dam workers were housed here, and although many of the buildings have disappeared, cottages 1–12 look much as they did when they were built.

10 Commercial District, Boulder City

Walk back into 1930s America. The arcaded, southwestern-style buildings were the precursors of today's shopping plazas. Boulder Dam Hotel, by contrast, is in southern colonial style.

Ancient Peoples

Archeologists disagree about how long humans have lived in the desert along the Colorado River. There were certainly people living downstream from the dam 3–4,000 years ago, and possibly as many as 8,000. The Patayans were among the first Native Americans known to live in the broader tri-state area (Nevada, Arizona, California), appearing in about 900 AD; they lived in brush shelters and ate pulverized seeds and plants. Their descendants split into the Hualapai and Mojave tribes.

5 Black Canyon River Raft Trips

The Colorado River flows lazily below the dam, so rafting is pleasant rather than of the white-knuckle variety. The trip takes a little more than three hours to make the 12-mile (19 km) trip to Willow Beach. Look out for petroglyphs carved in the rock, and ringbolts: in the days before the dam these were used to winch steam boats through Ringbolt Rapids.

8 Boulder City/Hoover Dam Museum

The dam and the people who built it are the focus of this museum, housed in the historic Boulder Dam Hotel (see p93, above). Don't miss the film chronicling the dam's construction. Memorabilia, photos, and posters give insights into life in the 1930s.

For more outdoor activities See pp56–7

TOP 10 Glitter Gulch

During the 1980s and early 1990s, as the Strip became ever more glamorous, the downtown area – including the stretch along Fremont Street known as Glitter Gulch – went further and further into decline. City fathers and casino owners alike agreed that something had to be done to reverse the process and took action to see that it was. The resulting efforts have revitalized the area. There is even a new hotel-casino under construction – the first to be built in the area in decades.

Fremont Street

🍴 For a memorable meal, try Florida Café Restaurante Cubano (1401 Las Vegas Boulevard S.).

⚠ Don't wander away from the bright lights after dark. High-crime areas still exist not far from Glitter Gulch *(see p131).*

Arrive a few minutes before the hour to see the light and sound show at the Fremont Street Experience. Then explore the shops and casinos or enjoy the stage entertainment until the next show begins.

• Map J–K4 • Golden Gate, 1 Fremont Street, 702 385 1906 • Golden Nugget, 129 Fremont Street, 702 385 7111 • Binion's Horseshoe, 128 E. Fremont Street, 800 237 6537 • Lady Luck 206 N. 3rd Street, 702 477 3000 or 800 523 9582

Top 10 Sights

1. Glitter Gulch Lights
2. Fremont Street Experience
3. Signs of the Past
4. Las Vegas's First Casino
5. Fremont Street Pedestrian Promenade
6. Golden Nugget
7. Binion's Horseshoe
8. Lady Luck Casino Hotel
9. Casino Characters
10. Entertainment

1 Glitter Gulch Lights

The heart of downtown has earned its name for reasons that become obvious as soon as you set foot here. This is one of the brightest places on earth – so much so that you can stand on the street at midnight and read a newspaper. Even before the Fremont Street Experience was conceived, the country's leading neon designers and lighting engineers were strutting their stuff here.

2 Fremont Street Experience

A major part of the down-town revival was the trans-formation in 1995 of one four-block stretch of Fremont Street into a pedestrian mall, covered with a 90-ft (27-m) high "Space Frame" containing more than two million lights. Every night, from 8pm until midnight, an hourly sound and light extrava-ganza entertains the crowds below. *(See also pp78–9.)*

Fremont Street Experience

3 Signs of the Past

Las Vegas Vic *(see p80)* has been waving to passersby on Fremont Street since 1951. More illuminating insights into the history of neon are at the Neon Museum on the corner of Fremont and Las Vegas Boulevard.

 For more on downtown Las Vegas See pp78–83

4 Las Vegas's First Casino

The place where it all started is the Sal Sagev Hotel on Fremont Street, which is now the Golden Gate. The strange-looking original name makes sense in mirror-writing. The new place is famous not so much for gambling as for its shrimp cocktails.

8 Lady Luck Casino Hotel

Lady Luck is best known for its "fun-books" (coupon booklets) which have been known to include such items as free foot-long hotdogs and free photos. The books are available at the casino's Mad Money booth.

6 Golden Nugget

The four-star Golden Nugget is the best-value hotel in the city (rates can fall as low as $60 in the off-season). Its casino is also first-rate *(see p37)*. Try the California Café for some of the best-value food downtown – and also for some great people-watching.

7 Binion's Horseshoe

The biggest names in poker play at the Horseshoe, and the annual World Series is held here each May. To compete for the million-dollar prize, contestants must ante (put up) $10,000. Dallas bootlegger and gambler Benny Binion established the property in 1951, and it is still owned by his descendants.

9 Casino Characters

If you ever want to get from one end of Fremont Street to the other, you will have to resist the charms of an assortment of exotically dressed showgirls, mermaids, and cowboys hired by the casinos to entice people in.

10 Entertainment

In addition to the production shows and lounge acts at most of the hotels *(see pp42–3)*, entertainment centers on Fremont Street. It's a popular venue for parades and performances by musical groups. (See also p82.)

Glitter Gulch Beginnings

For 20 years after its incorporation, entertainment in Las Vegas was limited to a few bars and brothels in the red-light district downtown. The legalization of gambling and arrival of 5,000 dam-construction workers in 1931 changed all that. Casinos opened on Fremont Street, and tourists began to arrive. World War II personnel and their families gave Las Vegas another population surge in the 1940s, and casino building continued apace after the war – as it does to this day.

5 Fremont Street Pedestrian Promenade

Another mid-1990s downtown improvement is the walkway between Main and 4th Streets, which is decked with flowers, colorful street vendors' carts, and strolling performers.

For the top hotels and casinos in Las Vegas **See pp32–7**

◉10 Bellagio

From the flower arrangements in the halls to the fixtures in the bathtubs, Bellagio Resort Hotel, built in 1998, is the epitome of perfection. The goal of Steve Wynn, who conceived this grand monument to leisure, was to create a hotel "that would exemplify absolute quality while emphasizing romance and elegance – romance in the literary sense, a place of ideal beauty and comfort; the world everyone hopes for, as it might be if everything were just right." Most everyone agrees that Wynn achieved his goal.

Façade of the Bellagio

⭐ For a leisurely lunch in a tranquil setting, reserve a table on the terrace at Olives, overlooking Lake Bellagio.

⭐ Take the monorail that runs between Bellagio and Monte Carlo. The ride through the extensive grounds of both resorts provides a few minutes of sightseeing and at the same time allows you to rest your feet.

To enjoy the full effect of Bellagio's fountain show, cross the street and go to the observation level of the Eiffel Tower at Paris Las Vegas.

• Map Q1–2 • 3600 Las Vegas Blvd S. • Reservations 888 987 6667
• General info 702 693 7111 • www.bellagio. com • $$$$$ (for price categories see p89)

Top 10 Features

1. Italianate Theme
2. Lobby Ceiling
3. Via Bellagio
4. Conservatory and Botanical Gardens
5. Casino
6. Gallery of Fine Art
7. Theater
8. Restaurants
9. Courtyard
10. Meeting and Business Facilities

1 Italianate Theme

Fronting on a pristine 8.5-acre lake with a tree-lined boulevard beyond, this extraordinary resort hotel was built to resemble an idyllic village on the shores of Italy's Lake Como. The Italianate theme is carried through the entire property – its 3,000-room tower, 16 restaurants, two wedding chapels, salon, and spa – imbuing the whole with an atmosphere of opulence. Creating this representation of Italy cost $1.6 billion.

2 Lobby Ceiling

Visitors are greeted by a dazzling 2,000 sq ft (186 sq m) garden of glass flowers – the Fiore di Como – suspended from the lobby ceiling. The creator was Dale Chihuly, the first American artist to be designated a national treasure; amazingly, every single flower is different.

For more theme hotels **See pp32–3**

Via Bellagio **3**

You are only likely to frequent Bellagio's shopping promenade if you have deep pockets. The establishments are as elegant as the Via itself, numbering among them such names as Prada, Tiffany & Co., Chanel, Giorgio Armani, Moschino, Hermes, Gucci, and Yves St Laurent. *(See also p52.)*

Casino **5**

Aesthetically this is the most pleasing casino in Las Vegas, less flamboyant and more sophisticated than the rest. Slot-machine carousels are fringed with specially designed fabrics rather than the ubiquitous neon tubing, and custom-made carpets provide a stylish relief from the norm.

Gallery of Fine Art **6**

Bellagio's art gallery hosts major temporary exhibitions of important international artists past and present in conjunction with other large art galleries and museums in North America and around the world.

Theater **7**

Designed for Cirque du Soleil's spectacular production "O" *(see p38)*, the theater combines Old World magnificence (it is styled after the Paris Opera) with cutting-edge technology. Central to the production is a 1.5 million gallon (6.8 million liter) pool, which can be remodeled to meet each act's needs.

Conservatory and Botanical Gardens **4**

Keen gardeners and plant-lovers who stay here regularly will be rewarded with floral displays that change with each season and every major holiday. Each change employs the services of no fewer than 150 professionals.

Restaurants **8**

Bellagio's superb restaurants include Le Cirque, Aqua, Noodles, Jasmine, and Shintaro. Picasso *(see p46)* holds the coveted Mobil five stars and is decorated with original Picassos.

Courtyard **9**

With its Italianate columns and statuary, six outdoor pools, and four spas *(see p65)*, the formal courtyard at Bellagio is glorious for morning and evening strolls. During the middle part of the day, it is transformed into a scene of poolside cabanas, chaises (sunbeds), and umbrella tables, with bronzed sun-worshipers sipping cool drinks.

Meeting and Business Facilities **10**

Bellagio has the capacity to host conference groups of up to 5,000 people in 10 different rooms, including two ballrooms. A professional staff is on hand to assist with needs such as word processing.

High Rollers

High rollers – gambling's big spenders – are courted by every major casino. Who qualifies (based on the amount he or she bets) varies a good deal, but a really big spender – someone who wagers thousands in an evening – will get superstar treatment from the top hotels. They may get flown to Las Vegas in a private jet, put up in a luxurious suite, and given carte blanche to order whatever they want from the hotel. Like superstars, high rollers are also treated with the ultimate discretion, so you may not spot one.

TOP 10 Grand Canyon

"Overwhelming" and "humbling" are the words most often used to describe the Grand Canyon experience. One of the world's most awesome sights, the canyon is 277 miles (443 km) long, 10 miles (16 km) wide and as deep as a mile (1.6 km) in places. Because of the vast differences in elevation between floor and rim, the canyon encompasses a range of desert and mountain habitats. The South Rim, easier to access via road than the North Rim, is a five-hour drive away from Las Vegas.

Layers of the canyon wall

⊜ See p106 for great places to eat at the Grand Canyon.

⟳ The South Rim of the Grand Canyon is accessible by road year-round, but the North Rim road and facilities are closed from November to mid-May.

You will need a permit to camp outside the official campsites within the national park. Apply in advance at the Backcountry Information Center.

• Map V2 • South Rim 271 miles (434 km), North Rim 255 miles (408 km) E of Las Vegas
• South Rim Visitor Center, Canyon View Information Plaza, Mather Point, open 8am–7pm daily, 520 638 7888
• www.nps.gov/grca
• Admission charge to enter national park $20 per vehicle or $10 per pedestrian

Top 10 Features

1. Flyovers
2. Lake Mead Access
3. Visitor Centers
4. Hiking and Mule Trips
5. Overlooks
6. Whitewater Rafting
7. Kaibab Squirrels
8. Tusayan Village
9. Golden Eagles
10. Purple Lupines

1 Flyovers

Airplane flights to the Grand Canyon rank among the most popular day trips from Las Vegas *(see p109)*.

2 Lake Mead Access

The most thrilling way to visit the canyon is via the river itself in your own canoe or raft. Begin the trip at Pearce Ferry, Lake Mead, ending 40 miles (65 km) later at the first rapids of Separation Canyon. You do not need a permit for this part of the river. If you have an outboard motor, you may be able to get there and back in a day. Otherwise, allow three or four days and camp along the way.

3 Visitor Centers

Information centers are located at the North and South Rims of the canyon, where you can pick up free area maps, orientation information, and *The Guide*, which describes facilities for disabled visitors and activities for children. The Grand Canyon Railway *(below)* runs from the town of Williams to Grand Canyon Village, close to the South Rim Visitor Center. Great observation points are near both centers.

For more on the canyon and places to stay **See pp98–109**

Hiking Trails 4

Ranking high with South Rim hikers are the South Kaibab, Bright Angel, and Rim trails *(see p108)*.

Popular North Rim day hikes include those along the North Kaibab, Angel Point, and Widforss trails. Don't attempt to hike to the canyon floor and back in one day: apply for an overnight permit.

Overlooks 5

For the grandest of the grand views, head for the Yaki, Grandview, and Moran Points on the South and East Rims. You should be able to see almost to Utah from the top of the 70-ft (23-m) Watchtower. Yavapai Observation Station and Maricopa Point have marvelous vistas. Motorists can use the Desert View Drive (Hwy 64) along the South Rim, following the edge for 26 miles (42 km). Hermits Rest Road hugs the North Rim for 8 miles (13 km), but is closed from October to May due to heavy snowfall.

Golden Eagles 9

About 3 ft (1 m) long and with a wingspan of 6–7 ft (2 m), golden eagles can often be spotted flying to and from their lofty aeries constructed on the canyon walls.

Purple Lupines 10

Lupinus hilii, the lovely species of lupine that graces the rocks of the Grand Canyon, is not found outside Arizona.

Whitewater Rafting 6

Dozens of companies offer whitewater rafting trips along the Colorado on the canyon floor. Trips vary in length from one day to more than two weeks *(see p109)*.

Kaibab Squirrels 7

Dark gray with white tails and tufted ears, Kaibab squirrels are found only on the Kaibab Plateau and North Rim of the Grand Canyon. Look out for these pine-cone-eaters in forested areas.

Tusayan Village 8

Ruins of rock dwellings inhabited by ancestors of the Hopi Indians for a short period around 1200 AD are preserved at Tusayan. On display at the adjacent museum are artifacts, models of recreated dwellings, and exhibits of contemporary tribes who live in the area. A feature entitled *Grand Canyon – The Hidden Secrets* is presented on a 70-ft (23-m) IMAX screen.

Exploration of the Canyon

In 1869, Major John Wesley Powell, a veteran of the American Civil War, led an exploration party along the Colorado River through the canyon. On August 28, three of the men left the group at the rim of Separation Canyon. They were killed by Native Americans. Ironically, it was the following day that Powell's expedition emerged safely from the gorge, completing the first exploration ever made of the Grand Canyon.

Following pages **The South Rim at dusk, Grand Canyon**

⑩ The Venetian

Some months after the opening of Bellagio (see pp14–15), Sheldon Adelson was ready to unveil the Venetian. Everyone held their breath. Could anyone possibly replicate Venice? Of course not: Adelson imitated this most romantic of Italian cities just enough to catch the flavor but without sacrificing Las Vegas pizzazz. Since opening, the Venetian has announced a number of added attractions – the Guggenheim Las Vegas, the Hermitage-Guggenheim, plus extra eateries. Venice? Not really. But exciting – definitely!

Arcade in the grounds of the Venetian

- 🍽 Splurge on a meal at Wolfgang Puck's **Postrio**, named by *Hotels Magazine* as "one of the ten greatest restaurants in the world."

- ⏱ It is almost as much fun – and a lot less expensive – to watch the gondoliers from land as it is to actually ride in the gondolas.

  If possible, visit the Venetian when there is a full moon and the crowds have thinned: by moonlight it is breathtaking.

- • Map P2 • 3355 Las Vegas Blvd S.
- • 702 414 1000
- • www.venetian.com
- • $$$$$ suites only (for price categories see p89)

Top 10 Features

1. Architecture and Ambience
2. Lobby
3. Grand Canal
4. St. Mark's Square
5. Canal Shoppes
6. Restaurants
7. Madame Tussaud's
8. Guggenheim Las Vegas
9. Hermitage-Guggenheim
10. Casino

1 Architecture and Ambience

The grandeur of Venice meets Las Vegas glitz, and the results are surprisingly spectacular. True, the Grand Canal is only 1,200 ft (350 m) long as opposed to two and a half miles (4 km), but any lack of authenticity is made up for by the festive Las Vegas ambience.

2 Lobby

Reproductions of frescoes framed in 24-karat gold adorn the domed and vaulted ceilings. Marble floors, classical columns, costumed courtiers, and a giant overview of the real Venice all serve to transport the imagination.

3 Grand Canal

Push the boat out and hire the Venetian's very own Wedding Gondola for your marriage ceremony! You can even sail under the Rialto Bridge.

5 Canal Shoppes

The galaxy of goodies in the shops along the canal *(see p53; left)* satisfy a wide range of tastes: there are magic tricks at Houdini's and ice-cream cones at Haagen Däzs; there are pearls at Mikimoto and smart sportswear at Banana Republic. Travel by gondola or meander the (rather long) walkway linking the stores.

6 Restaurants

Stars of the Venetian's gastronomic line-up include Wolfgang Puck's Postrio (Asian-Mediterranean cuisine), Emeril Lagasse's Delmonico Steakhouse, Stephan Pyles' Star Canyon (New Texas dishes), and Joachim Splichal's Pinot Brasserie (French-California fare).

7 Madame Tussaud's

In a building fashioned after the library on St. Mark's Square, the wax museum *(above)* opened in 1999 and soon became a top attraction; some visitors say the figures are even more lifelike than those in the London original. *(See pp28–9.)*

4 St. Mark's Square

So the geography isn't exactly as per the original, but even if you notice you probably won't care – the total effect is, aesthetically, extremely pleasing, perhaps more so than at any of the other new resorts.

8 Guggenheim Las Vegas

Completed in late 2001, this is the fifth of the world's Guggenheim museums *(see p44).* The others are in New York, Bilbao, Berlin, and Venice.

9 Hermitage-Guggenheim

Also established in late 2001, this is the first perm-anent museum outside St. Petersburg, Russia, to house treasures from the Hermitage *(see p45).*

10 Casino

Set in the Doge's Palace, the vast casino has 110 table games and 2,000 slot machines. On the walls of the high rollers' "Renaissance Room" hang works by Tiepolo, Tintoretto, and Titian. Costumed singers belt out arias in counter-point to the cacophony of slot-machine bells and clanging coins.

High Hurdles

The journey of a major hotel-casino from the drawing board to the grand opening is a long and often tortuous process. Of course, plans must be submit-ted and approved by city government and county commissioners. But the most rigorous scrutiny is reserved not for the building but for those involved in owning and managing the casino. These people are vetted by the Nevada Gaming Commission and subjected to a thorough background check before a gaming license is issued.

 For more on museums **See pp44–5**

Aladdin

Reopened in 2000, Aladdin hotel and casino megasresort bears the same name as its much humbler predecessor. Somewhat more expensive than the old Aladdin, the new one cost a cool $1.4 billion. The 50 ft (15 m) waterfall that tumbles down the faux-sandstone cliff at the entrance, the arches, and embellishments of the façade conjure images of exotic Arabian lands, which are echoed throughout the interior. One departure from the theme is the London Club, a posh casino within the casino for high rollers and VIPs.

Façade of Aladdin

🔊 Visit Desert Passage first. Check out the restaurants as you stroll and be sure to make dinner reservations at the one you like the look of best.

🕐 Don't miss the giant bird from Sinbad the Sailor guarding the Roc Bar.

Leave the laptop at home. Each room and suite at Aladdin has its own computer.

• Map Q2 • 3667 Las Vegas Blvd S.
• 702 785 5555 •
www.aladdincasino.com
• $$$$ (for price categories see p89)

Top 10 Features

1 Architecture and Ambience
2 Desert Passage
3 Theater for the Performing Arts
4 Blue Note Jazz Club
5 Commander's Palace
6 Josef's Brasserie
7 Sur la Table
8 Rickshaws
9 Exotic Shops
10 Casino

1 Architecture and Ambience

In Vegas, hotels rise phoenix-like, not from the ashes but from demolition sites. Aladdin is the city's most recent phoenix (the original opened in 1967). The whole is an Arabian fantasy of domes and minarets. Drawbacks are the somewhat confusing layout and the piped-in music that doesn't quite fit the theme, but the guest rooms are luxurious – each complete with its own personal computer.

2 Desert Passage

The most interesting shopping arcade in the city *(see p52; below)*, Desert Passage is divided into areas:

India Gate, the Lost City, Morocco Gate, and Merchants Harbor. The names are intriguing, and so are the shops. The architecture reflects the Arabian theme *(left)*, and, for added drama, realistic thunderstorms crash into the "harbor" every half hour.

22   For more theme hotels See pp32–3

3 Blue Note Jazz Club

Styled after the legendary jazz club in New York's East Village, the Blue Note in Las Vegas serves up contemporary jazz stars such as Spyro Gyra and the Dizzy Gillespie Alumni All-Stars, along with drinks and dinner.

4 Theater for the Performing Arts

The original Aladdin's Theater for the Performing Arts was saved from the surrounding demolition and incorporated into the new design. The renovated, state-of-the-art venue now hosts Broadway shows and major concerts by top stars (see p40).

5 Commander's Palace

Like its New Orleans parent, Commander's Palace Las Vegas is best known for its signature creole dishes such as turtle soup au sherry, and bread pudding soufflé. The decor recreates an Old South ambience with draperies and shuttered windows, ornate chandeliers, and potted palms.

6 Josef's Brasserie

At Josef's, the decor is casual French country, with hand-painted murals and large, ornately framed mirrors. The menu features traditional dishes such as *boudin blanc* (pork and chicken sausage), quiche Lorraine, and leg of lamb. Grand meal finales include bananas foster and peach melba. The oyster bar, with seafood flown in daily, gets rave reviews.

7 Sur la Table

In Desert Passage, Sur la Table is an outlet of one of America's best houseware chains. More than 14,000 items are stocked in the excellent Las Vegas store. Specialty foods such as fondue mix, unusual marinades, and luxury chocolates are popular, along with cookbooks, top-brand utensils, and kitchen furniture.

8 Rickshaws

Festively painted and decorated with flowers, rickshaws transport footsore shoppers along the cobbled and mosaic-paved streets of Desert Passage. You can hop on for free, but do tip – the service is provided by an independent company, and tips form the drivers' only income.

9 Exotic Shops

Several of the shops and boutiques in Desert Passage are far more exotic than the usual Las Vegas fare, selling artifacts imported from Africa and beyond.

10 Casino

The decorative touches of Aladdin's casino are as flamboyant as any in Las Vegas. The centerpiece is an enormous Aladdin's Lamp, which dwarfs the players on the casino floor below.

Casino Entrance

A Design Triumph

The Aladdin's unusual "stacked" design puts the hotel's lobby, restaurants, and casino on different levels. This allows panoramic views of the interior – up from the ground level lobby and down from the restaurant floor. The hotel does not have a central elevator core: instead, the elevators are spread out so that no guest room in the 40-story tower is more than seven doors from one. Best of all, it is not necessary to trek across hundreds of yards of casino floor to reach the elevators!

For more on shopping **See pp52–3**

Red Rock Canyon

About 225 million years ago, everything at Red Rock Canyon was covered by an inland sea. The escarpment, formations, and caves were created after that sea evaporated and wind and rain began sculpting the land. This remarkable desert region lies just 10 miles (16 km) west of Las Vegas. A conservation area since 1990, it is protected from the encroaching asphalt and grass of city expansion. The 13-mile (21-km) scenic road that loops off Hwy 159 provides a good overview, but the best way to explore this part of the Mojave Desert is on foot.

Desert lizard

🅾 Stop at one of the Einstein Bagels shops in Las Vegas for a picnic lunch to eat at the Willow Spring picnic area.

✪ Trails that are suitable for wheelchairs start from the Visitor Center, at Willow Spring, and the Overlook.

You will need a permit if you want to camp overnight or go rock-climbing at Red Rock Canyon. Apply at the Visitor Center.

Take the usual precautions when visiting a desert area *(see p133).*

• Map T2 • 20 miles (35 km) W of Las Vegas • Visitor Center, 1000 Scenic Drive, open 8am–5pm • 702 363 1921 • www.redrock canyon.blm.gov
• Admission charge $5

Top 10 Features

1. Red Rock Vista
2. Visitor Center
3. Hikes and Guided Walks
4. Desert Tortoises
5. Children's Discovery Trail
6. Petroglyphs and Pictographs
7. Thirteen-Mile Drive
8. Bookstore
9. Desert Whiptail Lizards
10. Tinajas

1 Red Rock Vista

The view from this overlook (about one mile past the Hwy 159 turnoff to the Canyon) is of the Red Rock escarpment itself, which rises a breathtaking 3,000 ft (1,000 m) from the valley floor. Time your trip to get here at either sunrise or sunset when the colors of this Aztec sandstone are at their sensational best.

2 Visitor Center

The Visitor Center *(below)* has area maps and staff on hand to answer questions. You can peer through telescopes on the viewing terrace at the detail of surrounding formations. A small museum contains geological and natural history displays.

Elephant Rock, Calico Hills

3 Hikes and Guided Walks

Of more than 30 miles (50 km) of hiking trails within the canyon, the most popular include those to Ice Box Canyon (it really is cooler there) and Oak Creek. Guided walks focus on aspects of the environment such as native wildflowers and the area's geology.

For more parks and preserves near Las Vegas See pp98–109

4 Desert Tortoises

Look out for brown-shelled tortoises, which, with their lifespan of up to 100 years, may outlive you. They dig burrows in the desert and spend at least 95 percent of their long lives below ground. Astonishingly, adult tortoises can survive for a year without water.

6 Petroglyphs and Pictographs

The area around Willow Springs contains some fascinating prehistoric rock carvings and paintings. The exact meaning of many of the incised and painted symbols is not known, but because the area's early inhabitants were hunters and gatherers, it is believed that many symbolize the procuring of food.

9 Desert Whiptail Lizards

Common to the western United States, these small lizards have pointed snouts and forked tongues, which help them eat termites, spiders, scorpions, centipedes, and other lizards. Recognize them by the four or five light stripes along the back, and yellow- or cream-colored belly with scattered dark spots.

10 Tinajas

Prevalent in the Calico Hills and at White Rock Spring, tinajas (or tanks) are naturally formed rock catchments for water. They serve as drinking basins for wildlife and so are good places to head for photo opportunities.

7 Thirteen-Mile Drive

The main scenic loop (above) is a one-way road taking in the Rainbow and Bridge mountains, and the Calico Hills. Designated stopping points for views are scattered along the way. Head for Willow Spring or Red Spring for picnic areas. Most of the hiking trails are accessible from car parks on the loop.

5 Children's Discovery Trail

Ask at the visitor center about their especially strong program for children, which includes educational funbooks and incentives for learning. Up near Willow Creek is the Children's Discovery Trail to Lost Creek. Less than a mile long, this fun round-trip highlights points of interest along the way. Pick up the free accompanying workbook at the Vistor Center.

8 Bookstore

The Visitor Center bookstore covers the local flora, fauna, and geology. Excellent Southwest-themed books for children include *Gullywasher* by Joyce Rossi and *Cowboy Country* by Ann Herbert Scott.

Mountain Biking

Designated mountain bike trails include the 41-mile (65-km) Red Rock-Wilson Cliff Loop, with a mile-long extension to the north peak vista at the top of Wilson Cliffs. The full ride takes five to eight hours to complete and is classed as very difficult, but the views of the Sandstone Bluffs and Red Rock Canyon lands are magnificent. Other rides include those totally within Red Rock, the Bristlecone Pine trail in the Spring Mountain Recreation Area, and one through Blue Diamond back to Las Vegas.

🔟 The Forum Shops at Caesars

"So many shops and so little time" is the complaint of most first-time visitors to the Forum Shops. Opals from Australia, an endangered species store, couturier clothes, and art galleries – there are 150 stores in all. The common areas of the complex are open 24 hours a day, so the savvy travelers who want to window shop and get close-up looks at the Forum's fountains and buildings will stroll its lanes in the wee hours of the morning.

Cheesecake Factory

🔵 Have lunch at one of the restaurants with a sidewalk café, from where you can watch the passing parades.

🔵 Pick up a map of the shops at the information center *(see p115).*

Walking from the parking garage to the shops is a shorter trek than through the enormous casino.

If you're visiting with youngsters, set aside some time to visit the child-pleasing Disney Store, Warner Brothers Studio Store, and FAO Schwarz.

• Map P1–2 • Caesars Palace Hotel, 3570 Las Vegas Blvd S. • Shops open 10am–11pm Mon–Fri, to midnight or later Sat & Sun • Dining reservations 702 731 7731 • www.caesars.com/palace

Top 10 Shops and Sights

1. Festival Fountain
2. Lost City of Atlantis
3. Sky Ceiling
4. Chinois Restaurant
5. Upscale Fashion Shops
6. FAO Schwarz
7. Planet Hollywood
8. Wolfgang Puck's Spago
9. 3-D Motion Simulator
10. Cheescake Factory

1 Festival Fountain
Focal point of the original group of Forum Shops, the Festival Fountain is guarded by four animatronic statues of Roman notables, who on the hour from 11am talk about the days of the Roman Empire. The production generated excitement when the center opened in 1992.

2 Lost City of Atlantis
Created in 1997, this attraction *(below)* is the centerpiece for the newer section of the Forum Shops. Atop the giant circular monument is a statue of Poseidon. Rare species of Atlantic Ocean fish swim in a 50,000-gallon aquarium, the focus of a feature presentation held every half hour from 11:30am.

The Sky above the Forum

3 Sky Ceiling
The domed ceiling of the Forum Shops simulates a constantly changing sky. The morning sun shines; afternoon clouds float by; evening stars twinkle.

4 Chinois Restaurant
Wolfgang Puck's Chinois offers an eclectic blend of Asian and French cuisine. Charcoal-grilled Szechuan beef, wok-fried lobster, and sizzling whole catfish are all prepared with a French twist. *(See also p47.)*

For more on shopping See pp52–5 & 116

Upscale 5 Fashion Shops

When the Forum Shops opened in 1992 with the three Vs (Vasari, Versace, and Vuitton) among them, a new era in Las Vegas shopping dawned. Gucci, Escada, Christian Dior, Fendi, Bernini, Armani, and Lalique also beguile.

FAO Schwarz
6 Walk through a huge Trojan horse to enter this toy store. Inside, the sheer volume of toys is overwhelming. Character dolls range from storybook favorites Eloise and Madeline to G.I. Joe and Harry Potter. Computer toys include Virtual FAO Baby and Virtual Playroom. A robotic puppy named Techno walks, talks, begs, sniffs, snores, and plays with his ball. Buttercup Hippo, the Big Piano Dance Mat, and the Tommy Hilfiger Dolls are sold only by FAO Schwarz.

Planet 7 Hollywood
This enormous restaurant is crammed with Hollywood memorabilia. Framed movie posters, celebrity photographs, costumes worn in famous films, and movie props make this café – according to its advertisements – one of the largest repositories for movie mementos in the world. California-style cuisine features out-of-the-ordinary sandwiches and salads.

Wolfgang 8 Puck's Spago
Spago was the first of the celebrity chef restaurants on the Vegas scene, starting the trend that is upstaging the city's traditionally famous buffets (see pp48–9) with upscale dining. Duck with roasted garlic polenta and other unusual combinations are among the rotating specials at this sophisticated dining spot.

3-D Motion 9 Simulator
Don special 3-D glasses to experience the amazing full effects of four rides here. One features a spaceship ride through the galaxy, another simulates a submarine race to the South Pole. The roller coaster thrill ride is not for people who suffer car sickness, and the timid should avoid the haunted graveyard ride. Tickets can be purchased individually or as a package.

Cheesecake 10 Factory
With more than 200 items on the menu, Cheesecake Factory has everything from hot spinach and cheese dip with tortilla chips, bruschetta, and Tex Mex eggrolls to Triple Chocolate Brownie Truffle Cheesecake. Entrées include a teriyaki chicken that incorporates banana slices, pineapple, and brown sugar.

Commerce or Entertainment?

In most US cities, shopping is an end in itself: go to the mall, make purchases, return home. In Las Vegas, however, shopping has the added dimension of being coupled with entertainment. The Forum Shops and a trio of the new hotels – Aladdin, Paris, and the Venetian – all have musicians, singers, mimes, and other performers strolling along the shopping arcades entertaining the crowds. It's all free and it adds to the glamour and excitement (see also pp52–3).

🔟 Madame Tussaud's Wax Museum

Everything about Las Vegas is larger than life. At Madame Tussaud's (within the Venetian Hotel) this is literally true – and the precise figure is two percent larger. Each waxwork figure in the museum is made marginally bigger than its real-life counterpart, because wax shrinks as it ages. For authenticity, many items of clothing and props were purchased at celebrity auctions. Rings on the figures' fingers are regularly cleaned; hair must be washed and makeup retouched. And, as with real people, the figures' clothes frequently need cleaning.

Madame Tussaud's entrance

🍴 For a quick lunch on the way there or back, try the Venetian's Food Court.

⏱ To avoid big crowds, arrive soon after the museum opens and visit the rooms in reverse order.

Save time for browsing around the gift shop: the merchandise is more imaginative than you might expect.

• Map P2 • St Mark's Library Building within the Venetian Hotel, 3377 Las Vegas Boulevard S
• www.madame-tussauds.com/site /lasvegas • Open 11am–7pm daily
• Admission charge $13.50 (no need to pre-book)

Top 10 Features

1. Frank Sinatra
2. Show-time Legends
3. The Big Night
4. Sports Celebrities
5. Rock and Pop
6. Behind the Scenes Glimpse
7. Finale
8. Souvenir Photos
9. The Building
10. The Gift Shop

1 Frank Sinatra

Before entering the "Show-time Legends" section of the museum, get acquainted with a young, slender Sinatra *(right)* performing on the stage of the old Sands Hotel. Recordings of Sinatra standards and other stage props enhance the 1950s mood.

2 Show-time Legends

Come face to face with your idols in a real spine-tingler of a room: eavesdrop on Louis Armstrong chatting with Ella Fitzgerald, and gaze without fear of reproach at Marilyn Monroe, tantalizingly real in a sequined dress.

Frank Sinatra

3 The Big Night

A Hollywood gala is the setting, and the guest list is as impressive as they come. Mingle with the likes of Arnold Schwarzenegger (positively huge at 2 percent larger than life), Shirley MacLaine, Whoopie Goldberg, Paul Newman,. and Elizabeth Taylor *(left)*; and yes, the hair *is* real.

For more museums See pp44–5

4 Sports Celebrities

They would never normally be gathered together in the same room, but at Madame Tussaud's you suspend disbelief. Rubbing well-muscled shoulders are stars of track and field, tennis court, and boxing ring. Even with the waxwork enlargement, Russian gymnast Olga Korbut still looks tiny.

9 The Building

Extending the copycat theme, and in typically grand Las Vegas style, the building itself is a small-scale replica of the library building on the Piazza San Marco in Venice.

10 The Gift Shop

The gift shop is almost as entertaining as the museum itself. You can choose a wig or a hat that makes you look like your favorite star (well, quite like) – great for kids or for costume parties. On a more serious note, there's a chocoholics' area, with chocolate body-frosting and other "choco-therapy" items.

6 Behind the Scenes Glimpse

It can seem a little creepy, but the painstaking process of making the waxwork models *(above)* is fascinating – from taking precise measurements of each celebrity to matching skin tones, dental impressions, eye, and hair color.

7 Finale

The somewhat anticlimactic finale is a state-of-the-art, multimedia, theatrical tribute to Las Vegas, featuring music, movie clips, and a special appearance by Elvis.

5 Rock and Pop

Some things get better as you get older: remember those teenage heartthrobs of yours? Here you can get closer than you ever managed to at a concert. Videos and wrap-around sound help bring the experience to glorious life.

8 Souvenir Photos

A must-have souvenir is a photograph of yourself alongside your famous (or infamous) idol. It's a great talking point with your more gullible friends back home.

Madame Tussaud

Born Anne Marie Grosholtz in Strasbourg, France, in 1761, the future Madame Tussaud inherited a collection of wax figures from her mother's employer when the latter died in 1794. Anne Marie married civil engineer François Tussaud and went to Britain, where she toured her collection for 33 years, finally setting up the exhibit in London. The original collection was destroyed by fire but has been revived in the form of the present London museum and several other versions around the world.

For more about the Venetian Hotel **See pp20–21**

Left **Mormon fort** Center **The Rat Pack** Right **MGM Grand**

Great Moments in Las Vegas Histor

1 1855: Mormons Establish a Trading Post

Inhabited for centuries by Native Americans, and encountered by Spanish explorers in 1829, the Las Vegas area was only permanently settled in 1855 when a group of Mormons, led by Brigham Young, established a trading post here.

2 1931: Gambling Legalized in Nevada

The relaxed gaming laws passed in the Silver State in 1931 encouraged widespread participation *(above)*. In reality, betting and gambling were already widespread and, in some forms, legal.

3 1935: Boulder Dam Dedicated by Roosevelt

The greatest hydroelectric project of the 20th century, the Boulder (later Hoover) Dam was begun in 1931 and completed four years later, at a human cost of 96 lives. *(See pp10–11.)*

4 1940s: Air Conditioning and Irrigation Arrive

The ability to keep buildings cool and the greening brought about by irrigation made the Nevada desert far more attractive to developers. In 1941 Los Angeles hotelier Tom Hull bought land three miles south of downtown for $150 an acre and built the 100-room El Rancho motel – a new concept in accommodation.

5 Christmas Day, 1946: Bugsy Siegel Opens the Flamingo Hotel

A handful of hotels and motels followed El Rancho, but only when mobster Benjamin "Bugsy" Siegel built the Flamingo Hotel was the hitherto Wild West feel of the town replaced with the Miami Beach style that was to become the hallmark of the Strip.

6 1960: The Rat Pack Comes to Town

The extravagant Flamingo was widely imitated in the 1950s, and entertainment was an important part of the new casinos' allure. Frank Sinatra performed at the Sands hotel in 1960, with friends including John F. Kennedy in the audience. From then on Vegas became a playground of the so-called Rat Pack (Sinatra, Sammy Davis, Jr., Dean Martin, Peter Lawford, Joey Bishop, *et al).*

7 1966: Howard Hughes Arrives

Hughes's Summa Corporation was a dominant player in the Nevada hotel/casino industry. Legend (which makes up much Las Vegas history) has it that the eccentric billionaire arrived in

For the top hotels See pp32–3

town one day by limousine and was whisked up to his suite at the Desert Inn, where he lived as a recluse for several years, with uncut fingernails and hair.

8 1990s: The Era of the Theme Hotels Begins

In the 1970s and 1980s the hotels became larger and more flamboyant. In 1991 the groundbreaking MGM Grand, Treasure Island, and pyramid-shaped Luxor launched the theme hotel in earnest.

9 1998: Bellagio Opens

Hotelier Steve Wynn set a new standard for Las Vegas hotels with the luxurious Bellagio (see pp14–15). The former owner of the Mirage hotel group (sold to MGM in 2000) is acknowledged as the creative force behind the modern resort concept.

10 2000: The New Generation of Resorts

Las Vegas is becoming synonymous with luxury. Four more grand hotels – the Venetian, Mandalay Bay, Four Seasons, and Paris Las Vegas – opened in 1999, followed by Aladdin in 2000. And Steve Wynn has announced plans to build a hotel even more luxurious than the Bellagio.

Bellagio Resort Hotel

Famous Residents

1 Jerry Lewis
The comedian who famously teamed up with singer Dean Martin still has a solo act in town.

2 Howard Hughes
The eccentric billionaire used his inheritance to make still more money in the film and airline industries before becoming a force in gambling.

3 Liberace
Wladziu Valentino Liberace – aka Mr Show Business – opened at the Riviera in 1955 and never looked back.

4 Clara Bow
Silent film star Clara Bow, who became known as the "It Girl," lived in Las Vegas with actor husband Rex Bell.

5 Wayne Newton
In 1957, 15-year-old Newton started at the Fremont; he is still performing in Las Vegas today.

6 André Agassi
Born in Las Vegas in 1970, Agassi rose to become one of the world's greatest (and most popular) tennis players.

7 Debbie Reynolds
The film star was also owner of a hotel-casino and museum of Hollywood memorabilia.

8 Robert Goulet
The actor/entertainer is a veteran of such hit Broadway musicals as Carousel and The Man from La Mancha.

9 Surya Bonaly
The former women's figure-skating champion now performs professionally.

10 Phyllis McGuire
The entertainer is fondly remembered as one of the singing McGuire Sisters.

For the top casinos See pp36–7

Left **The Venetian** Center left **New York–New York** Center right **Caesars Palace** Right **Excalibur**

Theme Hotels

1 The Venetian
Whether or not the Venetian really evokes accurate images of Venice is beside the point: the sum of the hotel's parts adds up to an aesthetically pleasing whole. *(See pp20–21).*

2 Caesars Palace
Caesars Palace opened in 1966 and was long the Strip's most opulent and, some would say, most ostentatious hotel. Times change, though, and Caesars recently was forced to put millions of dollars into renovations in order to keep up with new-comers. Cleopatra's Barge – a floating lounge – is still as it was, and the cocktail goddesses still wear toga-like costumes, but new statues have been erected on the front lawn, and the former show theater, Circus Maximus, has been updated. ⦿ *3570 Las Vegas Blvd S.* • *Map P1–2* • *800 634 6001* • *www.caesars.com* • *$$$$* (for price categories see p89)

Hard Rock Hotel

3 Mandalay Bay
With its theme of Southeast Asia, Mandalay Bay has lush tropical foliage, dotted with tiny pagodas and temples. In the lobby area, exotic birds call from wooden cages. The huge swimming complex as well as several of the shops and the popular "rumjungle" lounge *(see p42)* emphasize the theme. There is also an events center *(see p40)*. ⦿ *3950 Las Vegas Blvd S.* • *Map R1–2* • *877 632 7000* • *www.mandalaybay.com* • *$$$$*

4 New York–New York
The Statue of Liberty raises her torch over the busiest inter-section in Las Vegas. Nearby the Empire State, CBS, and Chrysler buildings rub shoulders with the Brooklyn Bridge, Grand Central Station, and the New York Public Library. Despite the architectural license, New York – New York is an exciting place with all manner of well-observed details.
⦿ *3790 Las Vegas Blvd S.* • *Map R1–2* • *888 696 9887* • *www.nynyhotelcasino.com* • *$$$*

5 Hard Rock Hotel
The huge guitar sign outside and an enormous chandelier with

Treasure Island

saxophone pendants clearly identify this as a Hard Rock enterprise. Throughout the public rooms are displays of rock-and-roll memorabilia. And you'll hear only one kind of piped music, of course.
🕭 4455 Paradise Rd • Map Q3 • 702 693 5000 • www.hardrockhotel.com • $$$$

6 Treasure Island
The sidewalk outside is wooden decking, with rope railings along the waters of Buccaneer Bay. Skull-and-crossbone door handles lead to the casino, where treasure chests, old maps, and other pirate gear continue the theme. In the shopping arcade, specialty candies are sold at the Candy Reef. Pirates pose for photos at Buccaneer Bay when they're not doing battle with HMS Britannia.
🕭 3300 Las Vegas Blvd S. • Map P2 • 702 894 7111 • www.treasure islandlas vegas.com • $$$$

7 Rio
A carnival atmosphere pervades this upbeat hotel-casino (see also pp36, 88, & 89). Its huge neon sign is unarguably the best in town. The only departures from the theme – special events such as a visiting "Treasures of Russia" exhibit – are so fabulous that no one seems to mind. 🕭 3700 W. Flamingo Ave • Map C4 • 800 752 9746 • www.harrahs.com • $$$

8 Paris Las Vegas
Alas, the City of Light has to lose something in translation to the City of Bright Lights. Even so, the Eiffel Tower model is impressive; the bicycle-riding delivery boy, and a cheery "bonjour" from valet-parking attendants are nice touches, too.

Paris Las Vegas

🕭 3655 Las Vegas Blvd S. • Map Q2 • 702 946 7000 • www.parislv.com • $$$$

9 Aladdin
Fans of the Thousand and One Nights will enjoy the new Aladdin. The adjacent Desert Passage shopping area extends the theme to ancient Arabian trade routes. (See pp22–3.)

Entrance to Aladdin

10 Excalibur
One of the first theme hotels (built in 1990), this is still a favorite with children. The legend of King Arthur and his Knights is the theme through the games arcade and on into the wedding chapel on the "Fantasy Faire" floor. 🕭 3850 Las Vegas Blvd S. • Map R1–2 • 702 597 7777 • www.excaliburlasvegas.com • $$$

Following pages **Caesars Palace and the Forum Shops**

Left **Arizona Charlie's** Center **Fiesta** Right **Harrah's Las Vegas**

Casinos

1 Rio
Cocktail waitresses in bright, flouncy costumes, an upbeat color theme, and friendly personnel make this casino a favorite with residents and visitors alike. The Rio also has the reputation of serving the best casino food in town. Video poker is the most popular game here, perhaps because mini-TV sets are mounted on top of some of the machines. *(See also p33.)* ☜ 3700 W. Flamingo Ave • Map C4 • 800 752 9746 • www.harrahs.com

2 Monte Carlo
The building reflects its European namesake, but the casino is typically Las Vegas, with the usual machines and table games. Monte Carlo's slot club is, however, superior to most; the air seems fresher than in most casinos, too. ☜ 3770 Las Vegas Blvd S. • Map Q2 • 800 311 8999 • www.monte-carlo.com

Monte Carlo

3 Regent Las Vegas
The casino at this sophisticated Southwestern-style resort is small. It is also relatively quiet. Best of all, when gamblers want a break, they have a choice of strolling through the lush gardens, eating at nine different restaurants, and browsing the art gallery and smart shops. ☜ 221 N. Rampart Blvd • Map A3 • 702 869 7777 • www.regentlasvegas.com

4 Santa Fe
With more than 1,700 slot and video-poker machines, the Santa Fe also has a large non-smoking area. People who suffer from claustrophobia in casinos will find relief here, where ceilings are high and small groups of machines are located near the main entrance. During gaming breaks, watch the skaters at the Santa Fe ice rink. ☜ 4949 N. Rancho Drive • Map A1 • 702 658 4949

5 Harrah's
One of the most respected names in the gaming industry, Harrah's has more than a dozen properties across the USA and offers value for money in service, food, and ambience. Harrah's also has one of the best slot clubs as far as prizes are concerned; the club card can be used at any Harrah's casino, so it works well for people who like to gamble wherever they vacation. ☜ 3475 Las Vegas Blvd S. • Map P2 • 702 369 5000

36

For more casinos See pp88 & 97

6 Hyatt Regency Lake Las Vegas

Because of the hotel's location, 17 miles from Las Vegas, most of the people who gamble here are hotel guests, so it is usually quiet during the day when many of them are playing golf. Even when full, the casino never feels crowded –

The Golden Nugget, Fremont Street

a great plus for people with a low tolerance for noise. ☉ 101 Montelago Blvd • Map H4 • 702 567 1234 • www.lakelasvegas.com

7 Fiesta

The decor is unmemorable, but the slot and video-poker machines are considered the most liberal in town. There's a drive-up sports book – gamblers can place bets without getting out of their cars. Eateries are close to the casino floor, so non-stop gamblers don't have to take much time out for eating. ☉ 2400 N. Rancho Drive • Map B2 • 702 631 7000

Sunset Station

8 Golden Nugget

This casino sets itself apart from its downtown neighbors, for both clientele and ambience. The restaurants are very good, and the casino provides a pleasant place to gamble while waiting to see the Fremont Street Experience (see p79), which takes place just outside its doors. ☉ 129 E. Fremont St • Map K4 • 800 846 5336 • www.goldennugget.com

9 Sunset Station

Primarily patronized by local residents, Sunset Station is located across from the Galleria at Sunset shopping mall. The casino is light and well-ventilated. It also has a Kids' Quest (nursery) on the premises. ☉ 1301 W. Sunset Rd, Henderson • Map F6 • 702 547 7777

10 Arizona Charlie's

Western-themed Arizona Charlie's is best known for its huge bingo parlor. There's also an enormous race and sports-book facility. As in most casinos that depend largely on the local trade, its employees are very friendly. ☉ 740 S. Decatur Blvd • Map B3 • 702 258 5200 • www.arizonacharlies.com

Left **Les Folies Bergère** Center **Lord of the Dance** Right **EFX**

Shows

1 "O"
" *O*", staged by Cirque du Soleil, is a circus quite unlike any other. The whole show revolves around the theme of water (hence the name, as in the French *eau*). Seven hydraulic lifts raise and lower the water levels throughout the performance, allowing for spectacular diving and other feats. ⊗ *Bellagio Hotel, 3600 Las Vegas Blvd S. • Map Q1–2 • 702 796 9999 for tickets*

Cirque du Soleil's "O"

2 Mystère
Created especially for Treasure Island, *Mystère* is an enchanting circus that – like all Cirque du Soleil productions – has a mystical thread running through it. The costumes are innovative and colorful. ⊗ *Treasure Island Hotel, 3300 Las Vegas Blvd S. • Map P2 • 702 796 9999 for tickets*

3 Lance Burton: Master Magician
Even people who don't usually care for magic shows wax lyrical about this one. Not only is Burton engaging, but his tricks are truly impressive. Children love this show: Burton invites them onto the stage to help him work his magic. The Victorian-style theater, designed especially for the show, is modeled on similar ones in London's West End. ⊗ *Monte Carlo Hotel, 3770 Las Vegas Blvd S. • Map Q2 • 702 730 7160*

4 EFX
The name is show-business shorthand for "special effects," which this show has in abundance. Star Rick Springfield rocks and rolls his way through a series of adventures in which he encounters Merlin the Magician, circus impresario P. T. Barnum, magician Harry Houdini, and the Brave New World of H. G. Wells. The 85,000-watt sound system feeds 300 loudspeakers, and the lights require enough electricity to power 1,400 average-size homes. ⊗ *MGM Grand Hotel, 3799 Las Vegas Blvd S. • Map R2 • 702 891 7777*

Mystère, Treasure Island Hotel

5 Lord of the Dance

This show takes Irish dance to dizzying new heights. Michael Flatley's variations on the traditional steps make the performances especially exhilarating. ◎ *New York – New York Hotel, 3790 Las Vegas Blvd S. • Map R2 • 702 740 6815*

6 Jubilee

Jubilee features showgirls who not only look good but also dance well. The show offers an effective mix of production numbers and specialty acts, glamorous costumes, and pretty tunes. There are terrific special effects, too, such as the sinking of the *Titanic*. ◎ *Bally's Hotel, 3645 Las Vegas Blvd S. • Map Q2 • 702 946 4567*

7 De La Guarda

The cast of the Buenos Aires-born show also write, compose, and choreograph this powerful production themselves. The show physically envelops the audience so that they become part of the action. ◎ *Rio Hotel, 3700 W. Flamingo Rd • Map C4 • 702 252 7777*

8 Danny Gans

Gans is a superb impersonator with a repertoire of 300 voices. It's a good show to combine with a trip to Madame Tussaud's *(see pp28–9)*! ◎ *Mirage Hotel, 3400 Las Vegas Blvd S. • Map P1–2 • 702 7796 9999*

9 Les Folies Bergère

The longest running show in Las Vegas began in 1979, a century after the Paris production hit the stage. Like the original, the Vegas show is predicated upon glamorous showgirls wearing spangles, sequins, and little else. The production numbers are lavish, the music tuneful. While the first show

Jubilee, Bally's Hotel

each evening is suitable for families, the second is topless. ◎ *Tropicana Hotel, 3801 Las Vegas Blvd S. • Map R2 • 702 739 2417*

10 Siegfried & Roy

Since 1990 when the show opened, animal trainers-cum-magicians Siegfried & Roy, along with their white tigers, have presented more than 5,000 performances. The tigers can also be viewed in their habitat *(see p72)*. ◎ *Mirage Hotel, 3400 Las Vegas Blvd S. • Map P1 • 702 796 9999*

Left **Thomas & Mack Center** Center **Le Théâtre des Arts** Right **Judy Bayley Theater**

🔟 Music and Performing Arts Venues

1 Hollywood Theater and Garden Arena

Headliners such as comedians Rodney Dangerfield and George Carlin, and music groups such as The Monkees, regularly appear at the 630-seat Hollywood Theater *(below)*. MGM's larger 15,200-seat special-events center, the Garden Arena, is used for superstar concerts, major sporting events, and other spectaculars. It was the setting for the much-publicized Barbra Streisand Millennium Concert on New Year's Eve 1999, for which tickets cost as much as $2,500. ⬡ *MGM Grand Hotel, 3799 Las Vegas Blvd S. • Map R2 • 800 646 7787*

2 Mandalay Bay Events Center

Luciano Pavarotti inaugurated the 12,000-seat events center in 1999. Since then, performers as diverse as tenor Andrea Bocelli (with the Russian Symphony Orchestra), Ricky Martin, and Bette Midler have graced its stage. During one month in particular, the Mandalay Bay Center was exceptionally eclectic, staging as it did a heavyweight bout between Evander Holyfield and John Ruiz, skater Katarina Witt's *Kisses on Ice* show, and Bocelli's vocal performance. ⬡ *Mandalay Bay Hotel, 3250 Las Vegas Blvd S. • Map R2 • 02 632 7777*

3 Theater for the Performing Arts

Since the new Aladdin Hotel opened in the summer of 2000, its theater has been the venue for such productions as *Forever Swing*, the Broadway musical *Fosse*, and *Les Misérables*, as well as a concert by British musical star Sarah Brightman. ⬡ *Aladdin Hotel, 3667 Las Vegas Blvd S. • Map Q2 • 877 888 5267*

4 Sam Boyd Stadium

The stadium hosts some of the biggest entertainment and sporting events in the country. Built in 1971, the seating capacity has been increased over the years: 40,000 spectators can now be accommodated. ⬡ *University of Nevada Las Vegas, 7000 E. Russell Rd • Map F5 • 702 895 3900*

5 Judy Bayley Theater

In addition to possessing excellent acoustics and comfortable seats, the Judy Bayley Theater features a special stage of flexible design. Primarily used for ballet, musical comedy, and dramatic productions, the theater also serves as home to the Nevada Dance Theater. ⬡ *University of Nevada Las Vegas, S. Maryland Parkway • Map Q4 • 702 895 ARTS*

 For more on entertainment **See pp118–19**

6 Artemis Ham Concert Hall

Across the courtyard from the Judy Bayley Theater, the Artemis Ham Concert Hall is an elegant building that serves as the venue for performances of both nationally and internationally acclaimed musicians and dancers. Violinist Itzak Perlman and the Bolshoi Ballet are among the star names that have appeared here. 🔊 *Map Q4*
• *University of Nevada Las Vegas, S. Maryland Parkway* • *702-895-ARTS*

7 Thomas & Mack Center

Named for two leading bankers who financed the project, Thomas & Mack's gala grand opening in 1983 was nothing if not star-studded, featuring as it did Frank Sinatra, Dean Martin, and Diana Ross. The center serves as the venue for rodeos, university basketball games, circuses, world championship boxing matches, and concerts. The record box-office takings for a single event were more than $6 million for the Holyfield vs Bowe heavyweight boxing bout in 1992; the record attendance for a single concert was 17,664.
🔊 *University of Nevada Las Vegas, S. Maryland Parkway* • *Map Q4*
• *702 895 ARTS*

8 Orleans Showroom

The 800-seat theater presents several headliners each month. The list of past performers is a veritable "who's who" of the entertainment world: Jerry Lewis; Willie Nelson; Peter, Paul, and Mary; Roy Clark; the Righteous Brothers; and Crystal Gayle, to name but a few. 🔊 *Orleans Hotel, 4500 W. Tropicana* • *Map B4*
• *702 365 7111*

9 Le Théâtre des Arts

The Parisian-style theater only opened in 1999, but in its short life has already played host to a some big names, including Dennis Miller, Bobby Vinton, Earth, Wind, and Fire, and the Moody Blues. 🔊 *Paris Las Vegas, 3655 Las Vegas Blvd S* • *Map Q2*
• *877 374 7469*

10 Clark County Amphitheater

This outdoor amphitheater is the setting for a popular and eclectic range of free public entertainment, from "Jazz in the Park" and moonlight concerts to folk festivals and barbershop quartets. The amphitheater's "brown-bag" lunches attract workers from nearby office buildings, Las Vegas residents, and visitors alike. 🔊 *500 S. Grand Central Parkway* • *Map K3* • *Events listed in local press*

Clark County Amphitheater emblem

Left **Studio 54 dancers** Center **VooDoo Café** Right **The Beach**

TOP 10 Nightclubs and Lounges

1 House of Blues

One of the city's most popular after-dark spots, House of Blues is a restaurant by day and a nightclub when no major concerts are booked. Flashback Fridays focus on music of the 1980s. A Sunday Gospel Brunch features a Southern-style buffet accompanied by live gospel music. There's live blues Thursday through Saturday – featuring such big-name entertainers as B. B. King, Sheryl Crow, and the Blues Brothers. Even if you don't like blues, visit just for the decor alone – the place is crammed with folk art.

House of Blues

⊗ *Mandalay Bay Hotel, 3950 Las Vegas Blvd S. • Map R1–2 • 702 632 7600* • *Admission charge*

Studio 54

2 Studio 54

Like its Manhattan namesake, Studio 54 attracts celebrities. Some of them even make impromptu stage appearances. Most nights, DJ Frankie officiates over the four dance floors and bars; special theme nights cater for different tastes. Additional entertainment is provided by performers suspended from bungees above the crowds. ⊗ *MGM Grand, 3799 Las Vegas Blvd S. • Map R2 • 702 891 1111* • *Open from 10pm Tue–Sat • Admission charge for men (free for women)*

3 Drais

Book-lined Drais is Las Vegas's only after-hours club. A fireplace, comfortable upholstered chairs, and potted palms add to the intimate atmosphere. With some of the world's greatest DJs playing everything from techno to Latin rhythms, the party usually goes on well after sunrise. ⊗ *Barbary Coast Hotel, 3593 Las Vegas Blvd S. • Map P2 • Open from 4am Fri–Sat, from 2am Sun*

4 rumjungle

Converts from restaurant to nightclub at 11pm Thursdays through Saturdays. Live bands are accompanied by dancers and gymnasts. ⊗ *Mandalay Bay Hotel, 3950 Las Vegas Blvd S. • Map R1–2* • *Admission charge*

For more on live music See pp40–41

club a favorite with the younger crowd. ◈ 365 Convention Center Drive • Map N3 • 702 731 1925

rumjungle

5 VooDoo Lounge
Smaller than the hotel's Club Rio, the VooDoo Lounge offers live music and a dazzling view of the Strip. There's a cover charge for guests not dining in the VooDoo Café. ◈ Rio Hotel, 3700 W. Flamingo Rd • Map C4

6 Baby's
This hip club features top national and international DJs in a subterranean setting complete with a vast aquarium. Music ranges from funky hip-hop to California techno. ◈ Hard Rock Hotel, 4455 Paradise Rd • Map Q3 • Admission charge for men (free for women)

7 Gilley's Dance Hall, Saloon, & Bar-B-Q
Gilley's offers a down-home atmosphere with Country and Western music. Free line-dance lessons precede the dancing proper on some evenings, "west-coast swing" lessons on others; some nights there's a live band. ◈ New Frontier Hotel-Casino, 3120 Las Vegas Blvd. S. • Map N2 • 702 794 8200

8 The Beach
With waitresses in bikinis and two floors decorated in an ocean and surfing theme, the Beach is a complete entertainment complex. Dancing, a restaurant, a sports bar, and a sports book make this off-Strip

9 Boston Grill & Bar
The Boston Grill & Bar is the only place in town that regularly features local bands. While the large, no-frills venue is lacking in atmosphere, the management's commitment in local music ensures that there are live acts at least five nights a week, ranging from punk and funk to rhythm and blues, swing, and soul. ◈ 3417 S. Jones • Map B4

10 The Armadillo Lounge
This north Las Vegas nightclub is noted for boot-scootin' (Country and Western) music and line dancing on Monday "Country Nights." On Sunday there's afternoon dancing to swing music; Wednesday and Thursday feature karaoke; Friday and Saturday you can hear the house band. ◈ Texas Station, 2101 Texas Star Lane • Map B2

Left **Madame Tussaud's** Center **Las Vegas Natural History Museum** Right **Elvis-A-Rama**

10 Museums

1 Guggenheim Las Vegas

Designed by award-winning architect Rem Koolhaas, this latest branch of the Guggenheim opened in autumn 2001. Larger than New York's Grand Central Station, the $21 million building includes a skylight with retractable panels painted as a replica of the Sistine Chapel ceiling. Traveling exhibits rotate with the other Guggenheims. ⓢ *The Venetian Hotel, 3355 Las Vegas Blvd S.* • *Map P2* • *Open daily* • *Admission charge*

Pavarotti, Madame Tussaud's

2 Madame Tussaud's Wax Museum

One can easily become so entranced with the wax figures that their theatrical settings are ignored *(see pp28–9)*.

3 Lied Discovery Children's Museum

With more than 100 hands-on exhibits, this is one of the finest children's museums in the western USA.

Children can skip along the Musical Pathway, toe-tapping out their favorite tunes on giant piano keys, and can learn about science through entertaining games. Little tots especially love the Bubble Pavilion and Toddler Towers. ⓢ *833 Las Vegas Blvd N.* • *Map J5* • *10am–5pm Tue–Sun* • *Admission charge*

4 Liberace Museum

A fittingly flamboyant tribute to the king of kitsch. Don't miss (as if you could!) the customized cars – including a red, white, and blue convertible Rolls Royce – and pianos. Also on display are the trademark capes and sequined jackets, plus collections of objects from around the world, including a piano-shaped ring set with 260 diamonds. ⓢ *1775 E. Tropicana Ave* • *Map R5* • *10am–5pm Mon–Sat; 1–5pm Sun* • *Admission charge*

Lied Discovery Children's Museum

 For more children's activities See pp66–7

5 Elvis-A-Rama

This huge collection of Elvis memorabilia is said to be worth between $3 million and $5 million. "The King's" guitars and his 1955 Cadillac are on display, as are such memorable artifacts as his blue suede shoes. You'd be unlucky to miss one of the five-times-a-day complimentary live performances – but is it Elvis? ◈ *3401 Industrial Road • Map N2 • 9am–7pm daily • Admission charge*

6 Hermitage-Guggenheim

The inaugural exhibition in autumn 2001, *Masterpieces from the Hermitage and Guggenheim Collections*, featured works by such monumental artists as Monet, Cezanne, and Picasso. Located as it is at the Venetian Hotel, one would expect nothing less *(see also p21).* ◈ *The Venetian Hotel, 3355 Las Vegas Blvd S. • Map P2 • Open daily • Admission charge*

7 Las Vegas Natural History Museum

Highlights include the international-al wildlife room and a live shark exhibit. The children's hands-on exploration room is excellent, but the animated dinosaurs, with their horrendous roars, elicit equally loud cries from frightened toddlers. ◈ *900 Las Vegas Blvd N. • Map J5 • Open 9am–4pm daily • Admission charge*

8 Clark County Heritage Museum

This unusual museum has historic buildings relocated from various sites around the state, exhibited alongside contemporary local artifacts. ◈ *1830 S.* Boulder Hwy, Henderson • Map G6 • Open 9am–4:30pm • Admission charge

9 Las Vegas Art Museum

Housed in a $20 million contemporary-style southwest building, the museum is a repository for both national and international works. Local arts and crafts are well represented in the museum's gift shop. ◈ *9600 W. Sahara Ave • Map A3 • 10am–5pm Tue–Sat; 1–5pm Sun*

10 Guinness World of Records Museum

The hall of fame for the heaviest, fastest, and tallest. Local record-holders are Brad Rodgers, owner of the world's largest collection of shot glasses, and Peter Rosendahl, who holds 26 records for feats accomplished on unicycles. ◈ *2780 Las Vegas Blvd S. • Map M3 • Open 9am–6pm daily • Admission charge*

Dinosaur, Natural History Museum

Left **Rosemary's** Center **Aristocrat** Right **Pamplemousse**

TOP 10 Gourmet Restaurants

1 Andre's
Quintessentially French restaurant in a converted house. *Coquilles* St. Jacques, magret of duck, lobster sausage, and smoked goose breast are classics. Service is gracious, and Andre Rochat presides over the kitchen. ◈ *401 S. 6th Street • Map K4 • 702 385 5016 • $$$$$ (for price categories see p91)*

2 Pamplemousse
With rough-hewn beams, baskets of fresh flowers on the tables, and nooks decorated with pottery and copper cookware, Pamplemousse ("grapefruit" in French) resembles a dining room in Provence. Dinner begins with baskets of breads, crudités, hard-cooked eggs, and olives. Entrées include veal medallions in a dijon-accented cream sauce, and roast duckling in a red wine and rum sauce. ◈ *400 E. Sahara Ave • Map M3 • 702 733 2066 • $$$$*

3 Picasso
The room is exquisite, with original Picassos on the walls and a carpet designed by Pablo Picasso's son, Claude, underfoot. Spanish-born chef, Julian Serrano, creates contemporary French dishes with an Iberian accent. Among the delights are sautéed medallions of fallow deer, a warm lobster salad, sautéed foie gras, and roasted langoustines. ◈ *Bellagio Hotel, 3600 Las Vegas Blvd S. • Map Q1–2 • 702 693 7223 • $$$$$*

4 Renoir
A feast for both the palate and the eyes, with lovely opening touches such as *rillettes* of salmon and ciabatta, which come unbidden to the table. The signature dish is braised beef short ribs with horseradish potatoes. The decor is enhanced by Renoir originals. ◈ *Mirage Hotel, 3400 Las Vegas Blvd S. • Map P1–2 • 702 791 7223 • $$$$$*

Picasso

5 Rosemary's
An extensive menu features the likes of rosemary roasted lamb with black olive mashed potatoes and grilled wild king

For more great places to eat See pp48–9, 82, 90, 96 & 106

salmon on a granny smith apple cabbage slaw with candied walnuts. Scrumptious desserts, include lemon ice-box pie with raspberry sorbet. The paintings on the walls are by local artists and are for sale. ✆ *125 W. Sahara Ave • Map M1 • 702 869 2251 • $$$$*

6 Chinois
If you read through the whole menu you may never get around to eating at Chinois – the sushi section alone lists 35 choices. Sizzling whole catfish and sweet soy-glazed Atlantic salmon are prepared with a French twist. ✆ *Forum Shops at Caesars, 3500 Las Vegas Blvd S. • Map P1–2 • 702 737 9700 • $$$$$*

Café Nicolle

house-smoked salmon on shredded potato pancake or the eggplant layered with provolone. ✆ *600 E. Warm Springs Rd • 702 944 7243 • $$$*

7 Renata's
An unusual mix of Asian, French, and Italian flavors. Stars include *escargot bourguignonne*, steak with stir-fried vegetables, and stuffed chicken breast with spinach, sun-dried tomato, fontina cheese, and marsala sauce. Save room for the chocolate truffle cake. ✆ *Suite 1, 4451 Sunset Rd, Henderson • Map D5 • 702 435 4000 • $$$$*

Renata's

8 Café Nicolle
A smart black-and-white decor with lipstick-red accents plus one of the nicest terraces in the city provide the backdrop for equally fine food. French crêpes, Italian *osso buco*, and a Greek spinach pie are among the highlights. ✆ *4760 W. Sahara Ave • Map M2 • 702 870 7675 • $$$*

9 Wild Sage Café
An innovative menu, reasonable prices, and lots of parking space make this a happy find for people who relish fresh ingredients artfully prepared. Try the

10 Aristocrat
Diners won't be disappointed at this cozily quaint and very British restaurant. Food is continental with dishes like mussels, beef Wellington, and veal Oscar on the menu. The fresh fish entrées are also good choices. In lieu of dessert, opt for an Irish coffee. ✆ *840 S. Rancho Drive • Map C2 • 702 870 1977 • $$$*

Left and center **Fresh Market Square Buffet** Right **Carnival World Buffet**

🔟 Salad Bars, Buffets, and Brunches

1 Village Seafood Buffet
This buffet was an instant success when it opened in 1997 and continues to be a favorite with local residents. Lobster tail, shrimp, clams, and other seafood are flown in fresh daily and kept fresh in saltwater; the seafood Mongolian barbecue is especially good. ✆ Rio Hotel, 3700 W. Flamingo Rd • Map C4 • 702 252 7777 • $$

2 Carnival World Buffet
Half the fun here is watching the chefs work as they interpret the flavors of Brazil, the East, Italy, Mexico, and the USA in a staggering 1,000-recipe repertoire. ✆ Rio Hotel, 3700 W. Flamingo Rd • Map C4 • 702 252 7777 • $$

3 Sterling Brunch
This may be the most expensive brunch in town, but the Sterling Brunch can compete with any in the world for quality and imagination. Two dozen appetizer choices include prosciutto mousse on raspberries,

caviar with warm blinis, and lobster gazpacho. Roast salmon in phyllo pastry with shrimp and spinach mousseline is the carving station star, while French toast with cinnamon ice cream provides a delicious finale. Reservations required. ✆ Bally's, 3645 Las Vegas Blvd S. • Map Q2 • 702 739 4111 • $$$

4 Regent Las Vegas Brunch
Located on the resort's second floor, the circular dining room provides seating on various levels, creating an unusual sense of space. Choose from around three dozen entrées and an ample array of main courses. The price ($18) rises to $25 on Friday and Saturday nights, when lobster is added to the gastronomic lineup. ✆ Upstairs Market Buffet, Regent Las Vegas, 221 N. Rampart Blvd • Map A3 • 702 869 7777 • $$

5 Sweet Tomatoes Salad Bar
The cool green and white interior plus extras like custom-made omelets and stuffed potato distinguish this salad bar from its rivals. The choice of dressings is extensive, and the ingredients are garden-fresh. The homemade chili is divine. ✆ 375 N. Stephanie St • Map E6 • 702 648 1957 • Another branch at 2080 N. Rainbow Rd • $$

Sweet Tomatoes Salad Bar

For more on eating out See pp82 & 90

Golden Nugget Buffet

6 Fresh Market Square Buffet

The Harrah's group of hotel-casinos has a reputation for excellent food. Although the buffet offerings at the Fresh Market Square are not as unusual as those of some competitors, the standards of preparation and service are consistently high. Folks in the know go for the salads and extremely attractive desserts. *Harrah's, 3475 Las Vegas Blvd S.• Map P2 • 702 369 5000 • $$*

7 Treasure Island Buffet

Linguine, chow mein, and fried chicken share the buffet in this popular *smorgasbord* of Italian, Chinese, and all-American dishes. Lines are always long, so do your best to avoid peak times. *Treasure Island Hotel, 3300 Las Vegas Blvd S. • Map P2 • 702 894 7111 • $$*

8 Souper Salad

The murals of bountiful harvests along the wall sum up the big-eating philosophy of this chain of glorified salad bars. Help yourself to everything you can eat – soup, main-course salads, dessert – for an incredibly low $4.99. *4022 S. Maryland Parkway • Map P4 • 702 792 8555 • Another branch at 2051 N. Rainbow Blvd • $*

9 Golden Nugget Buffet

There are around 60 buffet rooms in Las Vegas, and most could not be described as aesthetically lovely. The setting of the Nugget, however, is just that. The dishes are pretty tasty, too: don't miss the fresh carved turkey and old-fashioned bread pudding. *Golden Nugget Hotel, 129 Fremont St • Map K4 • 702 385 7111 • $*

10 Brown Derby Brunch

Hollywood's legendary Brown Derby Restaurant was demolished in 1994, but reproductions of its famous caricatures hang in the Las Vegas version. An upscale restaurant during the week, it is the setting for an extravagant champagne brunch on Sundays. *MGM Grand, 3799 Las Vegas Blvd S. • Map R2 • 702 891 3110 • $$$$*

For price categories See p91

49

Left **Little Church of the West** Center **Couple at Viva Las Vegas** Right **Wedding helicopter**

🔟 Wedding Chapels

1 Bellagio Wedding Chapels

Bellagio's two chapels provide some of the most elegant and romantic wedding venues in Las Vegas. Both have a stained glass window behind the altar, while ornate lamps and chandeliers of amethyst and Venetian glass compliment the pastel shades of the furnishings. Personalized services are available for room reservations as well as both wedding and reception planning. ⓢ Map Q2 • Bellagio, 3600 Las Vegas Blvd S. • 702 796 9999

2 Viva Las Vegas

Don't let the humble, rustic interior cramp your style: the chapel has a selection of fancy costumes at your disposal, covering such themes as Egyptian, Beach Party, Victorian, Gangster, Western, and even Intergalactic. ⓢ Map L3 • 1206 Las Vegas Blvd S. • 702 384 0771

3 Little Church of the West

The Little Church opened in 1942, making it one of the oldest wedding chapels in town. It is a favorite with the stars: Zsa Zsa Gabor and George Saunders, Betty Grable and band leader Harry James, and model Cindy Crawford and actor Richard Gere have all graced its portals. ⓢ Map C5 • 4617 Las Vegas Blvd S. • 702 739 7971

4 Jewish Temples

Very few churches and synagogues – as distinct from wedding chapels – perform "walk-in" ceremonies. Marriage requirements vary from congregation to congregation. Contact Temple Beth Shalom or Temple Adat Ari El for more information. ⓢ Temple Beth Shalom (Conservative United), 1600 E. Oakey Blvd • 702 384 5070 • Map L4 • Temple Adat Ari El (Reformed), 3310 S. Jones Blvd • 702 221 1230

5 Christ Church Episcopal

This traditional Episcopal church is the closest one to the Strip. Bear in mind that churches in the Episcopal Diocese of Nevada require pre-nuptial meetings with the church's rector before a wedding can be performed. ⓢ Map M4 • 2000 S. Maryland Parkway • 702 735 7655

Guardian Angel Cathedral

6 Guardian Angel Cathedral

Just steps away from the dazzling, bustling Strip, the Roman Catholic cathedral is refreshingly spartan. The giant triangular mosaic decorating the façade depicts a guardian angel and three figures representing Penance, Prayer, and – perhaps most elusive of all – Peace. ⊛ Map N2 • 336 Cathedral Way • 702 735 5241

7 Canterbury Wedding Chapels

Create your own version of Camelot by renting period costumes and tying the knot in one of Excalibur's two medieval-style chapels. Vow-renewal services are also on offer for the already-wed. ⊛ Map R1 • Excalibur, 3850 Las Vegas Blvd S. • 702 597 7777

8 Double Happiness Wedding Chapel

Take your pick of an ideal setting for your wedding: this chapel can be decorated as an outdoor garden, a non-denominational church, or a Chinese Buddhist temple complete with prayer towers and other religious articles. After the ceremony, bride and groom can commemorate the occasion by ringing a special wedding bell. ⊛ Map N1 • Chinatown Plaza, 4215 Spring Mountain Road • 702 252 0400

9 The Little White Chapel

This chapel represents what for many people is the epitome of Las Vegas; it has acquired a reputation for hosting rather unusual weddings. It was here in the spring of 2001 that a mass wedding took place, officiated by multiple Elvises. For the bride and groom who are acting on mad impulse or whose hectic lives leave them only a few minutes to spare, the Little White Chapel offers the world's only Drive-Up Wedding Window. The window is open 24 hours a

The Little White Chapel

day, and no appointment is necessary. ⊛ Map L4 • 1301 Las Vegas Boulevard S. • 702 382 5943

10 Helicopter Ceremonies

A helicopter company and the Little White Chapel (living up to its reputation for the bizarre) collaborate to provide airborne weddings. The "chapel in a chopper" hovers above the Las Vegas neon while the nuptial knot is tied. ⊛ Las Vegas Helicopter, Inc. • 702 736 0013

Left **Canal Shoppes** Right **Belz Factory Outlet World**

TOP 10 **Places to Shop**

1 The Forum Shops at Caesars

The Forum Shops are laid out along pseudo-Roman streets within the Caesars Palace complex, characterized by two-story storefronts topped with statues of Roman senators. Along with wares from Europe, American design is featured at stores like Banana Republic, Ann Taylor, and the Disney Store. Ask for a map of the shops at the Convention and Visitors Information Center *(see p115)* before you put on your shopping shoes. *(See also pp26–7.)*

2 Via Bellagio

Simply walking along Via Bellagio *(see also p15)* is an unforgettable experience. The boutiques are so opulent as to be intimidating: even if you dare not step inside, then at least the entrances to Escada, Chanel, Gucci, and others are large enough to see inside. Tiffany's windows are especially dazzling during the holiday season.
⊗ *Within Bellagio Hotel complex, 3600 Las Vegas Blvd S. • Map Q1–2*

3 Desert Passage

Italian cashmere at Manrico, men's European designer apparel at Casablanca Clothiers, and Alegre are among the upscale clothing stores. A fresher breath in merchandising comes from shops such as Tommy Bahama, which captures the joie de vivre of the tropics. ⊗ *Within Aladdin Hotel complex, 3667 Las Vegas Blvd S. • Map Q2*

4 Fashion Show Mall

This upscale shoppers' paradise is currently being renovated and expanded and will incorporate a venue for fashion shows and other events.
⊗ *3200 Las Vegas Blvd S. • Map N2*

5 The Galleria at Sunset

The newest of the city's residential malls, Galleria offers department store shopping and down-to-earth services, such as

Desert Passage

shoe and jewelry repair, free jewelry cleaning, alterations and tailoring, hairstyling, film developing, gift wrapping, and postage stamps. ✆ *1300 W. Sunset Rd, Henderson • Map E5*

6 Belz Factory Outlet World

Internationally known brands such as Nike shoes and Calvin Klein clothing are among the almost 150 outlets in this ever-expanding mall. The discounts on goods can be astonishing – sometimes as high as 75 percent. Style-conscious parents should seek out the children's outfitters Oshkosh B'Gosh, Bugle Boy, and Carter's. The obligatory Vegas-style entertainment comes in the form of a giant carousel plus laser light shows presented hourly. ✆ *7400 Las Vegas Blvd S. • Map C6*

7 Canal Shoppes

Located on the second floor of the Venetian *(see pp20–21)*, the emphasis at Grand Canal Shoppes is on European elegance. Exquisite goods for sale include handmade Venetian lace, glass, and masks as well as silks, shoes, and jewelry from various European countries. Part of the pleasure of shopping at this mall is the ambience – not quite like the real Venice, but enjoyable nonetheless. ✆ *The Venetian Hotel, 3355 Las Vegas Blvd S. • Map P2*

8 MGM Grand Shops

For people who enjoy logo items, MGM Grand shops offer four stores – MGM Grand & Co., Lion Habitat Retail Shop, a Rainforest Café outlet, and Las

Vegas Harley Davidson (motorcycle-related merchandise). Other businesses include Photo Magic. ✆ *Part of MGM Grand complex, 3799 Las Vegas Blvd S. • Map R2*

9 Hard Rock Hotel Logo Shop

This is definitely the most stylish of the ubiquitous logo shops in

Las Vegas. The rock music-oriented merchandise transcends coffee mugs and walking billboard T-shirts. Their aloha shirts are smart; the leather backpacks are handsome. ✆ *Hard Rock Hotel, 4455 Paradise Rd • Map Q3*

Hard Rock Hotel

10 Bally's Avenue Shoppes

Shoppers enter Bally's Avenue Shoppes by way of Bally's Plaza, a space-age fantasy of palm trees, fountains, and neon columns. In between visiting the two dozen or so clothes shops and art galleries, you can keep tabs on the latest scores in sporting events around the world at The Race and Sports Book. The ice-cream parlor is a delight. ✆ *Part of Bally's Hotel complex • 3645 Las Vegas Blvd S. • Map Q2*

This is page 54 of the Las Vegas Top 10 book.

Left **Dice clock** Center left **Circus Circus ornament** Center right **Vegas puzzle** Right **Elvis glasses**

Souvenirs

1 Jigsaw Puzzles of the Strip

A pastime with no cash payout, but plenty of variety in terms of styles of puzzle and images of Vegas. The most popular are puzzles that piece together the Strip by night or form cartoon renditions of sights along the Strip. And since this part of Las Vegas is ever-changing, you may one day have a collector's item.

2 Personalized Poker Chips

The perfect souvenir for people who host their own card games. Personalized chips come in traditional colors (see p124), but can bear your name in place of a casino's name and logo.

Retro slot machine

3 Souvenir Photos

Have your picture taken dressed as a pioneer, a cowboy, or a showgirl. Or, if the fancy takes you, you can dress up in a medieval outfit. Alternatively, have your face substituted for a magazine-cover celebrity. The photos generally cost $25 or less and make fun mementos.

4 Elvis Sunglasses with Fake Sideburns

Although he didn't make much of a hit when he first appeared in Las Vegas in 1956, Elvis Presley has since been firmly associated with the Entertainment Capital of the World. Your career as an Elvis impersonator could start here, with a pair of these sunglasses and sideburns.

5 Dice-Decorated Clocks

Made of bright blue lucite, glittery gold plexiglass, brass, wood burls, or any other material known to man, these clocks – with dice marking the hours – fall into the genre of Las Vegas kitsch. Other tacky items include toilet seats inlaid with playing cards and poker chips, and tissue box covers with gaming motifs.

6 Books about Nevada

Las Vegas bookstores carry a large assortment of publications on the locale, including *The Nevada Trivia Book* by Richard Moreno, *A Short History of Las Vegas* by Myrick and Barbara Land, and several about slot machines by Marshall Fey (grandson of the inventor of the first slot machine). For fiction, try *Sweet Promised Land* or *A Cup of Tea in Pamplona* by the late Basque-American writer, Robert Laxalt.

7 Nevada-Made Gourmet Foods

The best-known Nevada-made edibles are Ethel M. Chocolates, created by Forrest Mars, a

Poker chips

member of the Milky Way, Mars, Three Musketeers, and M&Ms manufacturing family. For the more refined palate, try Mrs Auld's Sweet 'n' Spicy pickles, her scone mix, or brandied cherries; Davidson Teas are good, too.

8 Antique Slot Machines
Machines that date back to a little after 1895 – when Charles Fey invented the very first slot machine, *The Liberty Bell* – occasionally appear on the auction block. Designs range from high Victoriana to Art Deco, and the rarer antique models can cost several thousand dollars.

9 Show Programs and Logo Items
Each major Las Vegas show has a shop associated with it, usually located near the box office. Commemorative T-shirts and various production recordings are the most common items for sale. However, anything that can be sold will be sold, including magicians' equipment, Chinese circus plates, and logo-emblazoned bottle stoppers, skipping ropes, and yo-yos.

10 Cash
The ultimate item to bring home from a Las Vegas trip has got to be several suitcases of hard cash. Although there are more losers than winners at the slot machines, roulette wheels, and gaming tables, visitors occasionally hit big jackpots, such as those on Megabucks and Quartermania machines, netting them huge sums of money.

Picture-Perfect Photo Spots

1 Bellagio Conservatory
Arrange your subjects in front of the most gorgeous floral display. The skylights give good light *(see p15)*.

2 Venetian Gondola
Have someone in another gondola take the photo so you can be in it, too *(see p20)*.

3 Hard Rock Hotel Swimming Pool
Best taken from a hotel room to get the pool's guitar shape *(see pp32–3)*.

4 Terrace, Hyatt Regency Lake
Wonderful at sunset, when the hills and houses are bathed in a gold light *(see p37)*.

5 Madame Tussaud's
Have your loved one stand next to his or her favorite wax museum celebrity *(see pp28–9)*.

6 Brahma Shrine, Caesars Palace
This lovely shrine is supposed to bring good luck *(see p32)*.

7 Treasure Island Gangway
Either of the ships makes a delightful backdrop for your photos, or take a shot of the ships and village *(see p33)*.

8 Glitter Gulch Entertainers
Pair your subject with a celebrity impersonator, who will be pleased to pose for a tip *(see p13)*.

9 Treasure Island – Venetian Overcrossing
A great vantage point for photographing the Strip. ◈ Map P2

10 Desert Passage Pedicab
Pile into a pedicab with your friends and have a passerby snap the shutter *(see p22)*.

Left **High Roller Roller Coaster, Stratosphere** Right **Las Vegas Motor Speedway**

🔟 Thrill Rides and Simulators

1 Manhattan Express Roller

For those riders who dare to keep their eyes open during this white-knuckler, the Coney Island-style ride offers spectacular views of the Strip. The coaster route writhes, dips, dives, and loops around the resort's perimeter. ® New York–New York, 3790 Las Vegas Blvd S. • Map R1–2

2 Big Shot

Located on the world's tallest observation tower, the Big Shot shoots riders 160 ft (50 m) into the air. They then freefall back to the launch pad. It's not a ride for the faint-hearted, or for kids – fortunately for them, though, there's a child-size version of Big Shot at Stratosphere. ® Stratosphere Tower, 2000 Las Vegas Blvd S. • Map L–M3

Star Trek

3 Star Trek: The Experience

This innovative simulation plunges participants into the 24th century. Having assumed the identity of a Starfleet or alien crew member, they go speeding across the galaxies, encountering the enemy along the way. Hungry space travelers can dine on 24th-century cuisine at Quark's Bar and Restaurant. ® Las Vegas Hilton, 3555 Las Vegas Blvd S. • Map N3

4 High Roller Roller Coaster

This is one of two Stratosphere thrill rides that are a

Big Shot, Stratosphere

dizzying 100 storys above the Strip. ❧ Stratosphere Tower, 2000 Las Vegas Blvd S. • Map L–M3

Indoor Skydiving

5 Canyon Blaster

At the Circus Circus theme park are some fun rides: try the water-flume ride through rushing water called the Rim Runner, and Twist and Shout, which involves riding rubber rafts through twisting tubes. The most exciting is Canyon Blaster billed as "the only double-loop, double-corkscrew indoor roller coaster." ❧ Circus Circus, 2880 Las Vegas Blvd S. • Map M–N3

Roller coaster, Sahara Speedworld

6 Sahara Speedworld

Surely the closest one gets to being launched into outer space without actually doing it. The "slingshot" electronic technology launches passengers on "Speed," the aptly named roller coaster. A 360-degree loop and a vertical climb of a 225 ft (68 m) tower (both forward and backward) add to the excitement – and it's all over in 48 seconds. ❧ Sahara Hotel & Casino, 2535 Las Vegas Blvd S. • Map M3

7 Race for Atlantis

Billed as the only IMAX 3-D ride on earth, this simulation takes participants on a race to save the doomed mythical kingdom. Climb aboard a "chariot" for a wild ride through all manner of hair-raising environments. ❧ Caesars Palace, 3570 Las Vegas Blvd S. • Map P1–2

8 Bungee Jumping

A. J. Hackett Bunjy (the premises are next to Circus Circus) has been in business 12 years with a reassuring 100 percent safety record. Jumpers go by elevator to the top of a (very) high tower, get strapped into safety harnesses, take a numbing look at the Strip 175 ft (53 m) below, and – well, jump. ❧ 810 Circus Circus Drive • Map M2

9 Indoor Skydiving

Flyaway Skydiving advises potential customers that skydiving is not without risk. The experience includes training and a simulated skydive in a wind tunnel. ❧ Flyaway Indoor Skydiving, 200 Convention Center Drive • Map N3

10 Richard Petty Driving Experience

After instruction, participants get into the driver's seat of an authentic Winston Cup-style stock car, and go, go, go!
❧ Las Vegas Motor Speedway, 6975 Speedway Blvd • Map E1

For more activities for children See pp66–7

Left **Powerboat racing, Lake Mead** Right **National Finals Rodeo**

🔟 Festivals and Annual Events

1 Chinese New Year
Chinese New Year festivities center around Chinatown Plaza *(see p85)*. Highlights include the traditional Chinese lion dance, firecrackers, foods, and *feng shui* as it pertains to the New Year. ⊗ *Chinatown Plaza, Spring Mountain Rd • Map B4 • Jan 21–Feb 19*

2 St. Patrick's Day Parade and Celebration
St. Patrick's parties are held at various restaurants and bars, with the parade and main celebration at the Fremont Street Experience. Crowd-pleasers include the Las Vegas Highland Pipe Band, entertainment on two stages, green beer (with green food coloring), and traditional Irish dishes. ⊗ *Map K4 • Mar 17 or closest weekend*

3 Cinco de Mayo
The Mexican national holiday commemorating the victory of the Mexicans over the French in 1862 is celebrated by the entire Las Vegas Hispanic community, including people from Central America and Cuba. Bands play everything from *ranchero* to rock. *Piñatas, mariachis*, carnival rides, and games, as well as food vendors selling *tamales*, tacos, and flan add to the festivities. ⊗ *Freedom Park • Map D2 • May 5 or closest weekend*

4 Snow Mountain Powwow
Tribal dancers in costumes decked out with beadwork, bones, shells, and bells come from across North America to perform ritual dances handed down from their ancestors. Feathered shields and foods such as Navajo tacos and fry bread are sold. ⊗ *Paiute Indian Reservation, 20 miles N • May*

5 Clark County Basque Festival
Events during this festival pertaining to all things from the Basque culture of northern Spain include a Catholic mass; feats of strength such as chopping huge logs in half and carrying heavy weights; and traditional dancing. Basque food is in abundance, and the *picon* punch is potent. ⊗ *St. Viator Community Center, 4320 Channel 10 Drive, Clark County • 702 361 6834 • Sep*

6 Pacific Islands Festival
The many Pacific Rim peoples who live in the Las Vegas area celebrate their various heritages one day each year with continuous entertainment, cultural exhibits, and fashion boutiques. Food includes everything from *kim-chee* and *poi* to potstickers and teriyaki. ⊗ *Lorenzi Park, 333 W. Washington Ave • Map C2 • Sep*

Tournament golf

7 Hallowe'en Haunted Houses

A group of professional magicians create haunted houses in parking lots, community centers, and parks. The "Texas Screamer" haunted house comes complete with mad doctor's laboratory and a surprise visit from the Texas chainsaw lunatic. ✪ *Late Oct*

8 Strut Your Mutt

No matter their pedigrees – or lack thereof – every dog has his day when the Strut Your Mutt competition takes place. There's the Mutt Parade and competitions to find the best dressed dog, the one with the most spots, and the one who can do the silliest tricks. ✪ *Dog Fanciers' Park, 5800 E. Flamingo Rd • 702 455 7506 • Nov*

9 National Finals Parties and BBQ Cook-Off

During the National Finals Rodeo, all of Las Vegas seems to go country – wearing jeans and boots. Casinos bring in country music bands, and line-dancing is enacted. The venues change from year to year, including that of the barbecue cook-off. The free entertainment magazines are the best sources of information about what's going on where. ✪ *Various venues • Dec*

10 Festival of Trees and Lights

Opportunity Village, an organization that helps the mentally challenged, raises funds by creating a Magical Forest with 50 decorated Christmas trees. The centerpiece is Santa's Castle, fashioned by the toy wizards FAO Schwarz. ✪ *Opportunity Village, 6300 W. Oakey Blvd • 702 259 3700 • Throughout Dec*

Sporting Events

1 National Finals Rodeo

Top cowboys compete for $4.2 million prize money at the country's premier rodeo. ✪ *Thomas & Mack Center • early Dec*

2 World Championship Boxing

Las Vegas is now the premier city for title bouts. ✪ *Caesars Palace, MGM Grand, Mandalay Bay, Thomas & Mack Center*

3 NASCAR Winston Cup Series

The Winston West motorcar race. ✪ *Las Vegas Motor Speedway • Dates vary*

4 Baseball

Watch the Las Vegas 51s on their home ground. ✪ *Cashman Field, 850 Las Vegas Blvd N. • Apr–Labor Day*

5 UNLV Sports Events

The university's Runnin' Rebels basketball, football, and baseball teams are frequently champions. ✪ *Thomas & Mack Center • Sep–May*

6 Ice Hockey

Las Vegas Thunder plays about 40 home games. ✪ *Thomas & Mack Center • Oct–Apr*

7 World Series of Poker

Poker players compete for $1 million. ✪ *Binion's Horseshoe Casino • Apr–May*

8 PBR Championship

Professional bull-riding competition. ✪ *Thomas & Mack Center • Last weekend in Oct*

9 Las Vegas Cup Powerboat Racing

Boats in various classes compete for prizes. ✪ *Lake Mead • Jun*

10 Las Vegas Invitational Golf Tournament

Famous for being Tiger Woods' first PGA championship. ✪ *Various courses • Mid-Oct*

Left **Jet skiing** Right **Cycling at Desert Shores**

Outdoor Activities

1 Hiking at Red Rock Canyon

Follow Hwy 159 (Charleston Boulevard) west for about 25 minutes to find yourself in another world *(above)*. A scenic drive loops through Red Rock Canyon: venture off this to feel truly miles away from civilization *(see pp24–5)*.

2 Cycling at Desert Shores

Cycling in Las Vegas can be pleasant – especially in the quieter, smarter residential areas of Green Valley and off Charleston Boulevard. Even better, though, are the paths at Desert Shores, in northwest Las Vegas, where you'll enjoy abundant shade and water views.

3 Jet Skiing on Lake Mead

Water babies should head for Calville Bay Marina or the Lake Mead Marina to rent jet skis, water skis, and other water craft. Note that the wearing of life jackets is obligatory out on the water. *(See pp92–5.)*

4 Roller-Blading at Summerlin

Summerlin is a planned community northwest of downtown, and its new, smooth sidewalks are perfect for roller-blading. The surroundings are among the most pleasant in the city, generally smog-free with attractive houses and condominiums; there isn't a lot of traffic either. In-line hockey fans should head for the rink at the Sports Park. ◈ *Las Vegas Sports Park, 1400 N. Rampart Blvd*

5 Tennis at Sunset Park

The eight floodlit courts at Sunset Park *(below)* are easy to get to (they are only about a mile from the southern end of the Strip), and they also cost far less than the courts at sports clubs and hotels. While you wait for a court enjoy the ringside view of planes coming in to land at McCarran International Airport. ⊗ Map D5

6 Skiing and Snowboarding at Mt. Charleston

Although the snow can't compare with that at famous resorts such as Aspen, Colorado, the skiing at Mt. Charleston can be

Ball games in Sunset Park

surprisingly good and makes a fantastic contrast with the golf and swimming options in the valley below. Ski lessons and equipment rentals are available in the Lee Canyon Ski Area, which is off Hwy 156. ⊗ 45 miles (72 km) NW of Las Vegas • 702 872 5408

7 Swimming at Northwest Pool

Although almost every hotel and motel in Las Vegas has a swimming pool, people who want to swim laps may find that there are too many other swimmers in the way. For a good pool workout, locals head for the eight-lane Northwest Pool. When you're bored with doing laps (or your children are bored with you doing laps), there is a 178-ft (54 m) spiral slide and an aquatic play gym. ⊗ 8601 Gowan Rd

8 Outdoor Basketball

There always seem to be pick-up basketball games in progress at either Desert Breeze Park or Sunset Park. The former has only two courts, but they are very new and of good quality. ⊗ Desert Breeze Park, 8275 Spring Mountain Rd • Sunset Park • Map D5

9 Strolling the Strip

Although there are dozens of paths off the beaten track, such as those at Arroyo Grande Park in Green Valley, most Las Vegas visitors do their strolling along the world-famous Strip. And why not? This road, actually a 3.5-mile (6-km) section of Las Vegas Boulevard South (or Hwy 604) is one of the most fascinating highways in the world. ⊗ Map M3–R2

10 Jogging at Sunset Park

If you're up to more than just a casual stroll down the Strip, one of the most popular joggers' venues is Sunset Park. Paths are well maintained and the circuit includes a fitness course. And there's plenty to look at to keep your mind off your feet: disc-golf courts, horseshoe pits, volleyball, and radio-controlled boating on the park's lake. ⊗ Map D5

For activities for children See pp66–7

Left **Las Vegas National Golf Club** Right **Angel Park Golf Clubs**

🔟 Golf Courses

1 Reflection Bay Golf Club

Nominated frequently by golf magazines as one of the top 10 courses in the USA, Reflection Bay, designed by the great Jack Nicklaus, follows one and a half miles (2.5 km) of the Lake Las Vegas shoreline. Great views of the lake and million-dollar hillside homes are an added bonus.
🚩 *75 Monte Lago Blvd, Henderson • Map H4 • 702 740 4653*

2 The Legacy Golf Course

The host to the US Open Qualifying tournament is a popular course with convention delegates, and combines Scottish links-style golf with the dramatic desert vegetation of Nevada *(below)*. The course highlight is the Devil's Triangle (holes 11–13). 🚩 *130 Par Excellence Drive, Henderson • Map E6 • 702 897 2187*

3 DragonRidge Golf Course

With its manicured fairways, bent-grass greens, and dramatic elevation changes, DragonRidge offers some of the most spectacular views in the valley. The course is private, with limited public play. 🚩 *552 S. Stephanie St, Henderson • Map E6 • 702 614 4444*

4 Bali Hai Golf Club

Just steps away from the Mandalay Bay and Four Seasons hotels, the course features thick stands of palm trees, large water hazards, tropical plants, and flowers in its South Seas design *(above)*. 🚩 *Las Vegas Blvd and Russell Rd • Map C5 • 702 450 8000*

5 Angel Park Golf Clubs

The Palm and the Mountain, this club's two 18-hole championship layouts designed by legendary American golfer Arnold Palmer, have been described as the "world's most complete golf experience." A night-lighted driving range, 18-hole putting course, and golf school form part of the complex. 🚩 *100 S. Rampart Blvd • Map A3 • 702 254 4653*

Angel Park

6 Las Vegas Paiute Resort

This was the first master-planned multicourse golf resort on Native American land. The Snow and Sun Mountain courses were designed by Pete Dye, who has designed 11 of the world's top 100 courses. ⊗ *Snow Mountain, near Mt. Charleston exit, 20 miles (32 km) N of Las Vegas* • *702 658 1400*

7 Desert Willow Golf Club

This challenging course is carved from the foothills of the Black Mountains and surrounded by hazards and hilly terrain. ⊗ *2020 W. Horizon Ridge Parkway, Henderson* • *702 270 7008*

8 Las Vegas National Golf Club

Established in 1961, this was the scene of champion Tiger Woods' first PGA (Professional Golf Association) victory in the 1996 Las Vegas Invitational. Soft spikes are preferred (some Las Vegas courses prohibit spikes of any kind). ⊗ *1911 E. Desert Inn Rd* • *Map D4* • *702 270 7008*

9 Royal Links Golf Club

The course features holes inspired by famous holes on the Open courses in Great Britain. All the golf carts are equipped with GPS (Global Positioning Systems). ⊗ *5995 E. Vegas Valley Blvd* • *Map E4* • *702 450 8000*

10 The Revere at Anthem

Winding through three desert canyons, this course features natural changes in elevation and spectacular views of the Las Vegas skyline. The summer rates, as at many Las Vegas courses, are considerably lower than those charged at other times of the year. ⊗ *2600 Evergreen Oaks Drive, Henderson* • *702 259 4653*

For more outdoor activities **See pp60–61**

Left **Stone massage** Right **Grand Spa, MGM**

🔟 Spas and Health Clubs

1 Canyon Ranch Spaclub
Residents at the Venetian can enjoy the 100-plus spa services, including movement therapy, Watsu pools, and 20 different styles of massage. The huge facility is also open to non-residents Sunday through Thursday, as is the Canyon Ranch restaurant. ⊗ Map P2 • The Venetian, 3355 Las Vegas Blvd S. • 702 414 3600

2 Aquae Sulis Health Spa
Named for the Roman baths and settlement at what is now Bath, England, this luxurious spa's traditions are rooted in the benefits of ritual bathing and body treatments. Choose simply to "take the waters" or indulge in a Southwestern hot-stone massage. East Indian Siddha Vaidya therapies are also offered. ⊗ Map A3 • Regent Las Vegas, 221 N. Rampart Blvd • 702 869 7777

Mirage Spa and Salon

3 Mirage Spa and Salon
Feel your stresses and strains ebb away amid lush foliage and hanging vines. Furnishings in peach, rose, and turquoise shades add to the air of tranquility. The sky-lit Grand Court allows access to separate men's and women's spa facilities, an exercise room, and beauty salon. ⊗ Map P1–2 • Mirage Hotel, 3400 Las Vegas Blvd S. • 800 374 9000

4 The Spa at Caesars Palace
Recently redone in a style mirroring the glory that was Rome, the spa incorporates Roman baths and other touches of imperial luxury. In addition to the myriad treatments on offer for both men and women, there are weight-training facilities, a fitness center with climbing wall, and a yoga studio. ⊗ Map P1–2 • 3570 Las Vegas Blvd S. • 702 731 7776

5 Spa at Bally's
You may need to take an expert with you to explain the joys of the Belavi facelift massage system, Panthermal (it's a steam-bed body facial for women), Russian leaf-therapy body scrubs, and hot or body-temperature jet spas. For those with simpler tastes there are those good old standbys, the Swedish massage, saunas, and a steam room. ⊗ Bally's Hotel, 3645 Las Vegas Blvd S. • Map Q2 • 702 967 4111

Las Vegas Top 10

6 Spa at Monte Carlo

Topline furnishings and personalized service are hallmarks of this spa, which is a certified Reebok facility complete with a large gym. Helio-therapy, body wraps, body scrubs, facials, and a variety of

Spa Bellagio

massages are on the menu of services. ◈ *Monte Carlo Hotel, 15 Las Vegas Blvd • Map Q2 • 702 730 7777*

7 Grand Spa

It's worth investing in a three-day pass here, so that you can sample each of the Balinese, Hawaiian, and Javanese therapies, performed by sarong-clad attendants to the accompaniment of island background music. ◈ *MGM Grand, 3799 S. Las Vegas Blvd • Map R2 • 702 891 3077*

8 Spa Bellagio

This Italianate pampering palace combines the elegance of marble with cutting-edge fitness equipment. The spa's signature treatment is the LaStone Massage, which combines specially "harvested" stones prepared in a hydrobath with an energy-balancing technique to provide a thoroughly relaxing experience. Service is attentive. ◈ *Map Q1–2 • Hotel Bellagio, 3600 S. Las Vegas Blvd • 702 693 7111*

9 Las Vegas Sporting House

Yoga, tai chi, boxing, and other classes are offered along with spa facilities, state-of-the-art fitness equipment, and free childcare. The club is open 24 hours and is conveniently located a little more than one block from the Strip. ◈ *Behind Stardust Hotel, 3025 Industrial Rd • Map N2 • 702 733 8999*

10 Las Vegas Athletic Club

The Athletic Club is considered by Las Vegas residents to be one of the premier fitness facilities in the city. It contains all the usual gym equipment, plus virtual-reality exercise mach-ines, abdominal and cardio rooms, and childcare facilities. The rates are reason-able, too, and the surroundings scrupulously clean. ◈ *5090 S. Maryland Pkwy • 702 798 5822*

Left **Old West theme park, Bonnie Springs** Right **Bowling center and ice arena**

Children's Attractions

1 Wet 'n' Wild

This spectacular water playground *(above)* has a special children's area with scaled-down water slides and bouncing lily pads. The most popular feature is the "Fujifilm Blimp," complete with squirt guns and other watery toys. ◎ *2601 Las Vegas Blvd S. • Map M3 • Open 10am– 6pm daily (later in summer) • Admission charge*

2 Dolphin Show and Secret Garden of Siegfried & Roy

These two attractions come as a package. Watch the dolphins give a brief but characteristically perfect performance *(right)*, then go on a tour, which includes underwater viewing. The Secret Garden is an oasis of trees and greenery, with unusual residents, including an elephant, a snow leopard, panthers, Bengal tigers, and rare white lions. You are allowed to stay in the garden as long as you like. ◎ *Mirage Hotel, 3400 Las*

Vegas Blvd S. • Map P1–2 • Open 11am–5pm daily (Secret Garden closed Wed) • Free for children under 10; admission charge for others

3 Rainbow Theatre

Children will find the dramatizations of folk tales, children's classic plays, musical comedies, and fantasies such as *No One Will Marry a Princess with a Tree Growing Out of Her Head* absolutely riveting. Performances of several works are presented each year. ◎ *821 Las Vegas Blvd N. • Map J5 • Programs vary • 702 229 6553 • Admission charge*

4 Interactive Fountains

Quarter-size holes in a plaza at this residential shopping center unexpectedly spurt out water at regular intervals throughout the day. Bring your youngsters dressed in their bathing suits so they can play while you relax on the café terraces. ◎ *Green Valley Center, 4500 E. Sunset Rd • Map E5 • Free*

5 The Ice Gardens

It may be swimming weather outside, but kids who like to ice skate can cool off at the indoor Ice Gardens, where there are both hockey and ice skating rinks. Ice-skating queen Surya

Dolphin Show, Mirage

Bonaly works out at the rink when she is in town. ✪ 3896 Swenson Street • Map P4 • Open daily, hours vary • 702 731 1062 • Admission charge

6 Las Vegas Mini Gran Prix
Adult Gran Prix Cars, sprint karts, go karts, kiddie karts, plus the Dragon Coaster, Super Slide, and lots of arcade games make this a favorite off-Strip destination for Las Vegas kids as well as visitors. ✪ 1401 N. Rainbow Blvd • Map A2 • 702 259 7000 • Open 10am–10pm daily (to midnight Fri & Sat) • Admission charge

7 Scandia Family Fun Center
This is a miniature golf course with a Scandinavian accent – all the mini-buildings are patterned after those in Europe's northern lands. ✪ 2900 Sirius Avenue • Map N1 • 701 364 0700 • Admission charge

8 Bonnie Springs and Old Nevada
This Old West theme park, which is 45 minutes west of the Strip, may lack the slickness typical of others in Las Vegas, but its rough-and-ready charm usually wins the children over. Among the features they most enjoy are the staged gunfights, stagecoach rides, zoo, and stores with merchandise from the days of yore. ✪ Gunfighter Lane, nr Red Rock Canyon • 702 875 4191 • Open 10:30am–6pm daily • Admission charge

9 Orleans Bowling Alley
Las Vegas has a lot of bowling alleys, but the Orleans, which has no fewer than 70 lanes, is consistently voted the favorite in the annual news-

Lion enclosure, MGM Grand

paper poll. Reasons for its success include the spacious surroundings, numerous tables and chairs, state-of-the-art computerized scoring system, and a snack bar with a big choice of items.
✪ Orleans Hotel, 4500 W. Tropicana Avenue • Map B4 • 702 365 7400 • Open daily, hours vary • Admission charge

10 MGM Grand Lion Habitat
The pampered cats are bathed, dried, and groomed daily before being transported to the enclosure at the MGM Grand. Few children can resist the lure of baby animals, and lions are very special. When the cubs are old enough to leave their mothers, they can be watched in a special "nursery" where they play with toys – and with the humans who feed and care for them. ✪ MGM Grand, 3799 Las Vegas Blvd S. • Map R2 • Open 11am–11pm daily • Free

Following pages **Heart of the Strip**

AROUND TOWN

LAS VEGAS TOP 10

AROUND THE REGION

Left **Circus Circus** Center **Tower, the Venetian** Right **Fountains, Bellagio**

The Strip

WALK ALONG THE LAS VEGAS STRIP *and you'll see that some of the best things in Las Vegas life are free – especially when it comes to sightseeing and entertainment. It costs nothing to walk through the hotel-casinos, and you can window-shop to your heart's content in their shopping promenades. The hotel architecture makes for an attraction in its own right: where else would you find an Egyptian sphinx, a Polynesian paradise, and a medieval castle in the same block? In addition, almost every hotel-casino has some sort of free entertainment going on outside its doors.*

Circus Circus

Pirate battle at Treasure Island

🔟 Strip Sights

1. **Treasure Island Pirate Battle**
2. **Circus Circus**
3. **Fountains at Bellagio**
4. **MGM Grand Lion Habitat**
5. **White Tiger Habitat**
6. **The Forum Shops at Caesars**
7. **Imperial Palace Auto Collection**
8. **Shark Reef at Mandalay Bay**
9. **Paris Las Vegas**
10. **The Mirage Volcano**

Gondoliers, the Venetian

1 Treasure Island Pirate Battle

This free show, staged at the entrance to the Treasure Island hotel, is a huge favorite with children. It opens as a band of pirates climbs aboard their galleon with treasure chests and supplies. One of the crew scurries up the rigging with a spyglass and spots the frigate *Royal Britannia* sailing in the galleon's direction. In eight minutes of swashbuckling adventure, the pirates and men of Her Majesty's Royal Navy do battle (the Navy come off worse every time!). ✎ *Treasure Island Hotel, 3300 Las Vegas Blvd S.* • *Map P2* • *Performances every 90 minutes, afternoon and evening* • *Free*

2 Circus Circus

Over the course of almost 30 years Circus Circus has entertained hundreds of thousands of spectators with their impressive shows. Stars have included the Flying Farfans of Argentina, the miniature-bicycle rider Charles Charles of Paris, and Russian acrobat Valerie Akishin. With performances every half hour, you can pop back for different shows to catch a wide variety of acts. ✎ *2880 Las Vegas Blvd S.* • *Map M–N2* • *Performances every half hour, 11am–midnight* • *Free*

3 Fountains at Bellagio

More than 1,000 fountains perform a water ballet above Lake Bellagio, in defiance of the parched, baking desert that surrounds the city. Soaring as high as 240 ft (73 m) in the air, the cascading water is choreographed to classical music. Bellagio and the other properties in the Mirage group use incandescent lighting rather than neon, which helps make the Italian village surrounding the lake a lovely backdrop for the dancing waters. ✎ *3600 Las Vegas Blvd S.* • *Map Q1–2* • *Performances every half hour, 3pm–8pm Mon–Fri, 12pm–8pm Sat–Sun. Once every 15 mins 8pm–midnight* • *Free*

4 MGM Grand Lion Habitat

In keeping with MGM's lion theme *(below)*, the hotel has a glass viewing station in the midst of a lion enclosure, allowing you to stand face to face with the king of beasts. Three of the 30 or so animals, Goldie, Metro, and Baby, are descendants of the original Leo, who posed for the famous MGM movie logo. ✎ *MGM Grand Hotel, 3799 Las Vegas Blvd S.*

➜ *For more on shows See pp38–9*

Imperial Palace Auto Collection

5 White Tiger Habitat

These regal white tigers, extremely rare in their native Himalayan foothills, should be on every sightseer's itinerary. The magnificent creatures live at the home of their trainers, Siegfried and Roy, whose show has wowed audiences at the Mirage for more than 10 years. When they are not training or performing, the animals can be viewed in their specially designed all-white habitat (it makes them feel camouflaged and secure), complete with waterfalls and palm trees. ⊗ *The Mirage, 3400 Las Vegas Blvd S. • Map Q1 • Open 11am–5pm Mon, Tue, Thu, & Fri, 10am–3.30pm Sat–Sun • Admission charge*

6 The Forum Shops at Caesars

Listen in on conversations between the robotic statues of Bacchus, Venus, Pluto, and Apollo at the Festival Fountain, and watch a mini-drama

performed by another group of statues – Neptune and his feuding children – at the Atlantis Monument. Some of the shops, too, provide entertainment: for a little magic pop into Magic Masters; look out for a secret door leading to the replica of Harry Houdini's library. The Warner Brothers Studio Store features a video wall showing previews of new films and also has an area where youngsters can create their own cartoons. *(See also pp26–7.)*

7 Imperial Palace Auto Collection

Highlights of this impressive display of more than 200 classic, antique, and special-interest vehicles include Hitler's 1939 Mercedes, General Dwight D. Eisenhower's parade car, and Mussolini's 1939 Alfa Romeo. Although there is an admission charge, look out for free tickets at tourist-information stations and in entertainment magazines. ⊗ *Imperial Palace Hotel, 3535 Las Vegas Blvd S. • Map P2 • Open 9.30am–9.30pm daily • Admission charge*

8 Shark Reef at Mandalay Bay

It is truly awe-inspiring to wander within the special walkways of the 1.3 million-gallon (5.9 million-liter) tank and observe the thousands of weird and wonderful sea creatures swimming together. Look out for the arowana dragon fish – and, of course, 11 different species of shark. ⊗ *Mandalay Bay, 3950 Las Vegas*

Blvd S. • Map R1 • Open 10am–11pm daily • Admission charge

9 Paris Las Vegas

The Eiffel Tower and Arc de Triomphe are faithfully and impressively reproduced at Paris Las Vegas Hotel, albeit on a smaller scale than the originals. Buy fresh baguettes from a street vendor, and nibble to the strains of tunes by the great Maurice Chevalier, as interpreted by a wandering accordionist. ◐ *3655 Las Vegas Blvd S. • Map Q2*

10 The Mirage Volcano

With displays like this, it is hardly surprising that the Mirage, when it was built in 1989, is said to have triggered the 1990s hotel-building boom. The man-made, multimillion-dollar volcano *(below)* spews fire 100 ft (30 m) into the air every 15 minutes, every evening. Ingenious lighting and steam effects convey the drama of lava flows, while loudspeakers broadcast vivid sound effects. ◐ *The Mirage, 3400 Las Vegas Blvd S. • Map Q1 • Erupts 7pm–midnight • Free*

A Day on the Strip

Morning

🕐 Start with breakfast in the delightful Verandah Café at Four Seasons, which is within the **Mandalay Bay** hotel. Be glad you're not about to become someone else's breakfast as you gape at the specimens in the **Shark Reef**. While still at the Mandalay Bay, check out the **House of Blues** *(see p42)* and the collection of American folk art.

Head north up the Strip to the **Lion Habitat** at **MGM Grand** *(p71)* followed by a walk to the **Imperial Palace Auto Collection** (car buffs in your party may have to be removed forcibly!).

For lunch, cross over to Harrah's for the **Fresh Market Square Buffet** *(see p49)*.

Afternoon

At the **Forum Shops** you are liable to shed the shoppers in your party.

Next stop is **Treasure Island** for the **Pirate Battle** *(see p71)*, accompanied by a doughnut and coffee from the outdoor stand. This will fortify you for the hike to **Circus Circus** *(see p71; eat too many doughnuts and you may opt for the CAT bus that stops all along the Strip). Laugh at your stomach outline in the funhouse mirrors before opting to walk back down to the **Mirage** for the **white tigers**.

Cross the street to the Casino Royale, snag a window table, and watch the **Mirage volcano** erupt while you dine. For a nightcap, walk down to the Eiffel Tower at **Paris Las Vegas**, where you'll have a choice view for the **Bellagio Fountain Show** *(see p71)*.

Price Categories

For a standard, double room per night (with breakfast if included), taxes, and extra charges.

$	under $50
$$	$50–$100
$$$	$100–$150
$$$$	$150–$200
$$$$$	over $200

Above **Caesars Palace**

🔟 Hotels

1 The Big Theme Hotels
The five largest and most extravagant hotels are Bellagio *(see pp14–15)*, The Venetian *(pp20–21)*, Aladdin *(pp22–3)*, Mandalay Bay *(p32)*, and Paris *(p33)*. Smaller than these, but still extraordinary in their dedication to a theme, are Caesars Palace *(p32)*, New York – New York *(p32)*, Treasure Island *(p33)*, and Excalibur *(p33)*.

2 Tropicana
Island music, exotic birds, and waterfalls make this complex a tropical paradise. ✪ *3801 Las Vegas Blvd S. • Map R2 • 800 634 4000 • www.tropicanalv.com • $$$*

3 Harrah's
Friendly hotel with comfortable rooms. It is also possible to play keno through the room's TV set. ✪ *3475 Las Vegas Blvd S. • Map P2 • 800 427 7247 • www.harrahs.com • $$$*

4 Circus Circus
A vast property with child-friendly attractions. ✪ *2880 Las Vegas Blvd S. • Map M–N2 • 800 634 3450 • www.circuscircus.com • $$*

5 Bally's
Relaxed atmosphere, an olympic-size swimming pool, and large, luxurious rooms, many with good views of the Strip. ✪ *3645 Las Vegas Blvd S. • Map Q2 • 800 634 3434 • www.ballyslv.com • $$$*

6 Stardust
A Las Vegas icon since it opened in 1958. Guests can stay in the hotel's towers or the Motor Inn, which has motel-style rooms with parking bays. ✪ *3000 Las Vegas Blvd S. • Map N2 • 702 732 6111 • www.stardustlv.com • $*

7 Mirage
Conveniently located in the center of the Strip, the Mirage is famous for its tropical atrium, pretty pool with cascading waterfall, and Siegried & Roy's white tigers *(see pp39 & 72)*. ✪ *3400 Las Vegas Blvd S. • Map P1–2 • 702 791 7111 • www.themirage.com • $$$$$*

8 Monte Carlo
An elegant European theme is reflected in the large rooms, each with a marble bathroom. ✪ *3770 Las Vegas Blvd S. • Map Q1–2 • 800 311 8999 • www.monte-carlo.com • $$*

9 MGM Grand
Despite being one of the largest hotels in the world, the Grand maintains a relaxed ambience. It boasts a luxurious spa *(see p65)*. ✪ *3799 Las Vegas Blvd S. • Map R2 • 800 929 1111 • www.mgmgrand.com • $$*

10 Luxor
Its 30-story pyramid and giant sphinx have been Vegas landmarks since 1993. ✪ *3900 Las Vegas Blvd S. • Map R1 • 800 288 1000 • www.luxor.com • $$*

For more theme hotels **See pp32–3**

Left **MGM Grand Arcade** Center **Games of the Gods** Right **Coney Island Emporium**

TOP 10 Game Arcades

1 Fantasy Faire
Traditional carnival attractions take on a new excitement with medieval knights racing around on their steeds. ⊗ *Excalibur Hotel, 3850 Las Vegas Blvd S. • Map R1*

2 Gameworks
Perhaps the noisiest place in town, Gameworks occupies a vast space on the lower level of the Showcase Mall, and offers more than 250 games as well as a restaurant and climbing wall. ⊗ *3785 Las Vegas Blvd S. • Map R2*

3 Games of the Gods
Also known as Segaworld, this is a favorite with local teenagers, for its virtual racing cars, flight simulators, and other tests of coordination; there are games for younger children, too. ⊗ *Luxor Hotel, 3900 Las Vegas Blvd S. • Map R1*

4 Caesars Garden of Games
In this strange juxtaposition of ancient Rome and modern Las Vegas, techno-warriors do battle amid fluted columns with sophisticated arcade games. ⊗ *The Forum Shops at Caesars, 3500 Las Vegas Blvd S. • Map P1–2*

5 MGM Grand Arcade
The huge arcade features the very best in video and virtual-reality games. ⊗ *MGM Grand Hotel, 3799 Las Vegas Blvd S. • Map R2*

6 Mutiny Bay
The arcade continues the pirate theme of the rest of the hotel; even the security guard is dressed for the part. ⊗ *Treasure Island, 3300 Las Vegas Blvd S. • Map P2*

7 Midway at Circus Circus
Games galore, plus an array of fun mirrors, hotdog stands, popcorn machines, and other carnival delights. ⊗ *Circus Circus Hotel, 2880 Las Vegas Blvd S. • Map M–N2*

8 Coney Island Emporium
Try out Big Apple-themed versions of traditional games such as coin pitches and shooting galleries, with New York-style food close at hand. ⊗ *New York – New York Hotel, 3790 Las Vegas Blvd S. • Map R2*

9 Monte Carlo Arcade
This arcade seems less hectic than most – a boon to anxious parents watching over their charges. ⊗ *Monte Carlo Hotel, 3770 Las Vegas Blvd S. • Map Q1–2*

10 In-Room Video Games
Most major Strip hotels will rent or loan video-game equipment to guests with children. Since by law no child under the age of 12 should be left unsupervised in a game arcade (and there is also a curfew for under-18s), many parents want to take advantage of this useful service.

For more on activities for children See pp66–7

Left **Treasure Island** Right **The Forum Shops, Caesars Palace**

TOP 10 Free Entertainment

1 Treasure Island
Top of the bill is the spectacular pirate battle staged regularly at the hotel entrance *(see p71)*. ✪ *Treasure Island, 3300 Las Vegas Blvd S. • Map P2*

2 Caesars Palace Grounds
When Caesars Palace opened in 1966, no one had ever seen anything quite like it. The grounds, studded with Roman-style statuary, were – and still are – enchanting. ✪ *Caesars Palace, 3570 Las Vegas Blvd S. • Map P1–2*

3 Paris Las Vegas
It may not be *quite* the real thing, but well-observed touches lend the place a characteristic *joie de vivre (see p73)*. ✪ *Paris Las Vegas, 3655 Las Vegas Blvd S. • Map Q2*

4 The Venetian's Gondoliers and Minstrels
The gondoliers sing as they pole their boats, and when not on the water they roam the casino harmonizing Italian arias. ✪ *Venetian Hotel, 3355 Las Vegas Blvd S. • Map P2*

5 MGM Grand Lion Habitat
Ferocious roars sound a warning as you approach the glass viewing tunnel *(see p71)*. ✪ *MGM Grand, 3799 Las Vegas Blvd S. • Map R2*

6 Mirage Volcano
This is Las Vegas at its lavish best: after dark, every 15 minutes, the "volcano" at the Mirage blows its top *(see p73)*. ✪ *Mirage Hotel, 3400 Las Vegas Blvd S. • Map P1–2*

7 Desert Passage Harbor Gate Rainstorm
This is certainly one of the city's more unusual attractions: an indoor rainstorm falling on a 155-ft (50-m) merchant ship. ✪ *Desert Passage Shopping Mall in Aladdin Hotel, 3667 Las Vegas Blvd S. • Map Q2*

8 Outside Elevator
Shaped like a giant Coca-Cola bottle, the elevator doubles as a people-watching and sightseeing opportunity. ✪ *Showcase Mall, 3875 Las Vegas Blvd S. • Map Q2*

9 M&Ms World
Extraordinary as it seems, an entire attraction – including a 3-D movie – has been built around these tiny, candy-coated chocolates. ✪ *Showcase Mall, 3875 Las Vegas Blvd S. • Map Q2*

10 The Sphinx at Luxor
It would be a shame (if hard) to miss the 10-story sphinx (larger than the original) guarding the Luxor Hotel-Casino. The best view of this Las Vegas landmark is as you come in to land at McCarran International Airport. ✪ *Luxor Hotel, 3900 Las Vegas Blvd S. • Map R1*

For more free entertainment **See p82**

Left **Mirage Volcano** Center **Fountain show, Bellagio** Right **Central Park, New York–New York**

TOP 10 Places to People-Watch

1 Bellagio Lobby
Settle down on a sofa to watch the gold dripping from the jet set. Soothe your envy with piano music from the caviar bar, Petrossian, and the marvelous artistry of the ceiling. ◈ *Bellagio, 3600 Las Vegas Blvd S. • Map Q1*

2 Benches at Desert Passage
Too much shopping is bad for the feet. So sit yourself down on one of those inviting benches in Desert Passage, and watch the world go by; the best ones are near Cashman Photos. ◈ *Aladdin Hotel, 3667 Las Vegas Blvd S. • Map Q2*

3 Around the Casino Tables
The stars play at upscale casinos such as MGM Grand, Bellagio, and Caesars Palace; stargazers should aim, apparently, for 11pm to 1am on weekends.

4 Mon Ami Gabi
Take a table at the sidewalk café, soak up the atmosphere, and enjoy the view of Bellagio's fountain show. ◈ *Paris Las Vegas Hotel, 3655 Las Vegas Blvd S. • Map Q2*

5 Treasure Island, Venetian, and Bellagio–Bally's Footbridges
Hop across Las Vegas Boulevard without playing traffic roulette, and enjoy marvelous vantage points of the mêlée below. ◈ *Map P2–Q2*

6 Central Park
The hotel's public area echoes famous New York City spots; the casino currently ranks as a top spot with the younger crowd, and they dress to be seen. ◈ *New York–New York Hotel, 3790 Las Vegas Blvd S. • Map R1–2*

7 Film Locations
Do some detective work on where the stars are each day by calling 702 486 2727. This number will tell you the daily casting calls and where filming is taking place.

8 Fiber-Optic Signs
An increasing number of supersize signs like the one at MGM are appearing on the Strip. Look up at one of these to gain a new perspective on your fellow men. ◈ *MGM Grand, 3799 Las Vegas Blvd S. • Map R2*

9 Studio 54
Even celebrities have to eat: serious star-hunters should book a table at Studio 54 nightclub *(see p42)* or one of the city's gourmet restaurants *(see pp46–7)*. ◈ *MGM Grand, 3799 Las Vegas Blvd S. • Map R2*

10 Forum Shops at Caesars
The cafés, benches, and slot-machine seats within the shopping complex are good for relaxation and people-watching *(see pp26–7)*. ◈ *Caesars, 3500 Las Vegas Blvd S. • Map P1–2*

Left **Glitter Gulch lights** Right **Pawn Shop Plaza**

Downtown

THE LAS VEGAS DOWNTOWN *is not a place of megastory financial temples. Instead, it is a conglomeration of government buildings, carnival attractions, not-so-very-glamorous casinos, storefront shops dealing in souvenirs, and unclaimed pawn shop miscellany.*
Glitter Gulch is the heart of the area, with its neon-lit row of casinos and, since the mid-1990s, free entertainment in the form of the Fremont Street Experience. This nightlife zone is here to stay, but the Las Vegas leadership is also planning a legitimate downtown on 61 acres close to Fremont Street, which will reflect the status of Las Vegas as one of America's richest cities.

Left **Fremont Street Experience** Right **Old Las Vegas Mormon Fort Historic Park**

10 Downtown Sights

1. Glitter Gulch
2. Fremont Street Experience
3. Downtown Casinos
4. View from Stratosphere Tower
5. Old Las Vegas Mormon Fort Historic Park
6. Pawn Shop Plaza
7. Bonanza Gift Shop
8. Vegas Vic Sign
9. World's Largest Slot Machine, Four Queens
10. Jackie Gaughan's Plaza Hotel-Casino Railroad Station

1 Glitter Gulch

The area called Glitter Gulch encompasses about eight blocks that front on Fremont Street between Main and Fourth Streets. Along this stretch is the most concentrated dazzle of neon on the planet. Not only are all the Fremont

View from Stratosphere Tower

Street casino fronts decorated with neon, but the street signs and light shows *(see p82)* above contribute to the dazzle. Nighttime, of course, is when the lighting is at its most intense. The crowds on the malled walkway are heavy until after midnight, and the entertainment adds to a feeling of carnival. *(See also pp12–13.)*

2 Fremont Street Experience

The part of Fremont Street associated with Glitter Gulch is now under cover and the site of lavish free entertainment collectively labeled the Fremont Street Experience. Alongside spectacular nightly sound and light shows *(see p82)*, special events take place throughout the year, such as the May talent showcase national finals, the June Las Vegas Jazz Festival, Summer in the City in July, the Rock and Roll Bandstand in August, Las Vegas Bikefest and Music Experience in September, Oktoberfest, and the Holiday Festival in December. § *Fremont St betwen Main and 4th • Map K4*

3 Downtown Casinos

Along with all the outdoor activity on Fremont Street, there's action inside the casinos, too. They may not be as glamorous as the big hotels on the Strip, but the Fremont Street and other

downtown clubs have more history – some date back to the 1940s. They are also known for their bargain meals.

4 View from Stratosphere Tower

You may not be able to see forever exactly, but, from the top of the tower on a clear day, parts of Arizona and California come into view. Count the 40 seconds it takes for the high-speed elevators to whiz up to the tower's floor-to-ceiling glass observation floor, which is 900 ft (275 m) above street level. The tower is a tourists' after-dark favorite for viewing the mesmerizing lights of Glitter Gulch and along the Strip. § *2000 Las Vegas Blvd S. at the corner of Main St • Map M3 • Free*

5 Old Las Vegas Mormon Fort Historic Park

Mormons built the fort, along with a trading post in 1855, as a defense against the Native Americans (who turned out to be peaceful). It is the oldest building of its type in Nevada, but of the original structures only a small adobe building that was part of the stockade remains. § *908 Las Vegas Blvd N. • Map J5 • Open 8:30am–4:30pm daily, except Christmas through New Year's Day • 702 486 3511 • Admission charge*

For more on Glitter Gulch See pp12–13

Glitter Gulch, with the illuminated icon, Vegas Vic

6 Pawn Shop Plaza

Chainsaws, boom boxes, fake Rolex watches, belt sanders, diamond rings, car jacks, and hundreds more items are piled on counters and hung from the ceilings in the shops of the plaza. This astonishing assemblage is testimony to the fact that some gamblers will sacrifice almost anything. Nevada law permits a monthly six percent interest on pawn shop loans – few pledges are redeemed. ⊗ *Area on First St north and south of the Fremont St intersection • Map J4*

7 Bonanza Gift Shop

The mother-of-all-souvenir-stores *(right)* includes such delights as miniature slot machine banks, X-rated bumper stickers, Elvis motifs on black velvet, sequin-studded hats, personalized dice, and gambling chip-encrusted toilet seats. The place is enormous, crowded with tourists, and crammed with anything that can possibly be marketed as a souvenir of the city. ⊗ *2460 Las Vegas Blvd S. • Map M3*

New Year's Eve in Glitter Gulch

Historically, Glitter Gulch has been the place favored by Las Vegas resident revelers for New Year's Eve. Each year since the advent of the Fremont Street Experience, the celebrations have become more elaborate with live music and other entertainment; food and beverages; a countdown to midnight; fireworks; and dancing in the streets. Of course, there are paper hats, noisemakers, and serpentines, too. But, unlike most Fremont Street happenings on all other days of the year, the New Year's Eve festivities are not free.

8 Vegas Vic Sign

Fifty feet (16 m) tall, Vegas Vic is a survivor from the early casino days. In bygone days not only did he smoke and wave but he also talked, saying "Howdy pardner, welcome to Las Vegas." Now, Vic's voice box works only sometimes, but he still provides the backdrop for thousands of visitors' photographs each year. ⊗ *25 Fremont Street • Map K4*

Mormon Fort

9 World's Largest Slot Machine, Four Queens

According to the Guinness World of Records Museum *(see p45)*, the enormous eight-reel contraption within the Four Queens Hotel-Casino is the largest slot machine in the world. Up to six players at a time insert from one- to three-dollar tokens into the slot of the 9-ft (3-m) tall and 18-ft (6-m) wide machine; an employee pulls the giant-size handle; and everyone watching holds their breath. Winning combinations are posted on the machine. Should you be tempted to try, bear in mind that the more reels a machine has, the more difficult it is to hit winning combinations. ⊗ *202 E. Fremont St.* • *Map K4*

10 Jackie Gaughan's Plaza Hotel-Casino Railroad Station

From Main Street, Jackie Gaughan's may look like just another casino, but if you walk on through you will find railroad tracks on the back side. The railroad station justifiably claims to be the only one in the world that is inside a casino, which was built around the existing Union Pacific Railroad depot in the 1970s. A map of the railroad's West Coast–Eastern Utah route is illustrated with an old-fashioned iron horse and a futuristic bullet train. Note that Main Street Station is further north. ⊗ *1 Fremont St at Main Street* • *Map J4*

Downtown After Dark

Late Afternoon

Begin your excursion in the mid- to late afternoon, with a flying visit to the **Mormon Fort** *(see p79)*. Allow more time if you are a history buff.

Next, head south to browse the **Bonanza Gift Shop**. Take a look around **Pawn Shop Plaza** while it is still light, then, as dusk deepens and the lights of Fremont Street begin to beguile, start exploring the **Glitter Gulch** nightlife *(p79)*.

Try dining at one of the top restaurants in downtown, such as Lily Langtry at the Golden Nugget Casino (129 Fremont St), with its black-and-white decor, or the romantic Hugo's Cellar at Four Queens (202 Fremont St).

Nighttime

After dinner, stroll along Fremont Street's pedestrian promenade, stopping in at the shops that catch your eye and the vendors' carts that capture your fancy. If gaming's your pleasure, step inside the El Cortez Hotel's casino (600 Fremont Street).

Check out the train station at the **Plaza**, then wander down to Main Street Station. Pick up a brochure here with a map and list of treasures – including street lamps from Brussels and a portion of the Berlin wall – that are incorporated into the building's decor.

Back at **Fremont Street Experience** *(p79)*, watch a light and sound show, then head to **Stratosphere** *(p79)* to top off the night with a stunning view of the city.

Left **Golden Gate shrimp cocktail** Right **Sport Club Hall of Fame**

🔟 Low-Cost Food & Entertainment

1 Fremont Street Experience

Six light and sound shows, *Heartbeat of a Planet*, *Las Vegas Legends*, *Dancing in the Street*, *Odyssey*, *Country Western Nights*, and *The Rescue* appear overhead on the hour until midnight in the arcade *(see p79)*. There are street performers and live music on mobile stages, too. ✪ *Map K4*

2 Noontime Concerts, Clark County Amphitheater

Many programs of marching bands, bluegrass and zydeco groups, country and western singers, and jazz quartets are free. ✪ *500 S. Grand Central Parkway • Map L3*

3 Golden Gate Shrimp Cocktails

For years, fresh shrimp cocktails have been the loss leader at the Golden Gate – they have sold 35 million so far. The cost: $1. ✪ *1 Fremont Street • Map K4*

4 Sport Club Hall of Fame

This free hotel-lobby museum includes bats swung by top baseball players and aerial views of major stadiums. ✪ *Las Vegas Club, 18 Fremont Street • Map K4*

5 Sam Boyd's Margaritas

Connoisseurs swear that the 99-cent margaritas, with just the right amount of salt rimming the chilled glass, are as good as any you can find elsewhere at many times the price. ✪ *200 Fremont Street • Map K4*

6 Steak Dinner at Binion's Horseshoe

From 11pm to 7am Binion's coffee shop serves a full New York steak dinner for $4.99. The line of diners begins forming at 10:15pm. ✪ *128 Fremont Street • Map K4*

7 Breakfast at Binion's Horseshoe

Two 24-hour-a-day breakfast specials are available at Binion's coffee shop for $4.50. One includes ham and hash browns; the other, pancakes. But wait: from 6 to 11am the club's snack bar sells scrambled eggs, sausage, and gravy for $2.75.

8 Golden Gate Hotdogs

All-beef frankfurters piled high with sauerkraut are served from a vendor cart in the casino's sports book (the lounge where people bet on sporting events). The hotdogs cost 75 cents.

9 Penny Video Poker Machines

The penny slot machines of the early casinos have disappeared from all but a few places such as the Gold Spike – you're more likely to spend 45 or even 90 cents with every pull. ✪ *Gold Spike Casino; 400 Ogden Avenue • Map K4*

10 Trolleys

The downtown trolley makes a regular circuit of Fremont, Ogden, and Steward streets daily from 7:30am–11pm. The fare is just 50 cents for adults.

Left **Vendor cart** Center **Desert Indian Shop** Right **Ray's Beaver Bag sign**

TOP 10 Places to Shop

1 Gambler's Book Club
Come here for volumes on slot machines, horse racing, card games, casino management, probability, and playing strategies. ⟨S⟩ 630 S. 11th Street • Map K5

2 Ray's Beaver Bag
Items recollect pioneer life in America, such as capes made of Hudson Bay blankets (called capotes), beaver skin bags, red flannel underwear, and black powder muskets. ⟨S⟩ 727 Las Vegas Blvd S. • Map K4

3 Stoney's Pawn Shop
The granddaddy of pawn shops, Stoney's is a treasure trove of unredeemed pledge items: a fascinating array of diamond rings, photographic equipment, musical instruments, and so on. ⟨S⟩ 126 S. 1st Street • Map K4

4 Gambler's General Store
An intriguing place even for non-gamblers, this huge store is devoted to gaming paraphernalia. There are dice tables, roulette wheels, antique slot machines, and the "shoes" from which cards are dealt in blackjack. ⟨S⟩ 800 S. Main Street • Map K4

5 Bonanza Gift Shop
The list of merchandise at this enormous store is as long as the souvenir manufacturers' imaginations. (See also p80.)

Stoney's Pawn Shop

6 Holy Cow! Gift Shop
Inside the black-and-white holstein-patterned building that houses the Holy Cow! Casino is a shop with hundreds of "cowllectibles." The bovine motif adorns everything from baby bibs to Christmas ornaments. ⟨S⟩ 2423 Las Vegas Boulevard S. • Map L4

7 Desert Indian Shop
Ninety-five percent of the merchandise is made by Native Americans, primarily members of the Zuni, Navajo, and Hopi tribes. Hand-crafted articles include Hopi *kachina* spirit dolls and Navajo rugs. ⟨S⟩ 108 N. 3rd Street • Map L4

8 Beef Jerky Store
Smoked salmon, roasted soybeans, dried plums, glazed apricots, and *biscotti* are sold alongside dozens of varieties of jerky (sun-dried meat). ⟨S⟩ 112 N. 3rd Street • Map J4

9 El Portal Indian Store
Native Americans produce and sell goods within the historic El Portal movie theater building. ⟨S⟩ 310 Fremont St • Map K4

10 Vendors' Carts
Carts placed at intervals down the center of the Fremont Street mall offer sunglasses, wind chimes, stuffed toys, baseball caps, and mini-cars in various makes and models. ⟨S⟩ Map K4

Left **Las Vegas Speedway** Center **Chinatown Plaza** Right **Henderson Farmers Market**

Beyond the Neon

LOOK BEYOND THE NEON *and you will find that Las Vegas is, like the god Janus, a two-faced town. One is about make-up and make-believe; the other is like that of other American towns, with more than 500 churches, first-rate community centers, parks, and playgrounds. Las Vegas is a city where significant research is undertaken at medical centers, and where cultural performances take place almost every night. It is also a growing city with many ethnic neighborhoods.*

Left **Botanical gardens, UNLV** Right **UNLV campus**

🔟 Sights Beyond the Neon

1. Chinatown Plaza
2. Foxcroft Park
3. UNLV Campus
4. Nevada State Museum
5. Ethel M. Chocolate Factory
6. Las Vegas Speedway and Carroll Shelby Museum
7. Masquerade Village Show in the Sky
8. Sunset Park
9. Marjorie Barrick Museum of Natural History
10. Henderson Farmers Market

Chinatown Plaza
1 With pagoda-style roofs, a traditional Chinese entrance gate, and a statue of the mythical monk Tripitaka, with his companions – a pig, a soldier, and a monkey – Chinatown Plaza offers a delightful blend of East and West. Stores specialize in both American and Eastern necessities and Asian luxuries. Chinese music wafts through the covered walkways (a misting system keeps shoppers cool in summer). Good stops include Chong Hing Jewelers, Valley Oriental Art Works and Paintings, Marco Polo Furniture, and Chinatown Florist. Not surprisingly, the restaurants are the best in town for Asian cuisine. *4215 Spring Mountain Rd • Map B4*

Foxcroft Park
2 One of the most pleasant parks in the Las Vegas area, Foxcroft Park has been the setting every September since 1994 for the "Shakespeare in the Park" festival. Each year a different work by Shakespeare plays to sell-out crowds. The Green Show preceding each performance features mimes, jugglers, and madrigal singers. *Valle Verde Drive just north of Warm Springs Rd, Henderson • Map C2*

UNLV Campus
3 City residents' favorite areas for taking a walk include the campus of the University of Nevada Las Vegas, which was established in 1957. The university may not have any remarkable buildings, but there are shade trees, and in early evening the paths are blissfully uncrowded. Be sure not to miss the desert garden, which is lovely. *4504 S. Maryland Parkway • Map Q4*

Nevada State Museum
4 The Nevada State Museum system is one of the best in the United States, and its Las Vegas branch is well deserving of a visit. The emphasis is on the anthropology and natural history of southern Nevada, with dioramas containing stuffed bighorn sheep, cougars, and other impressive wildlife. On a totally different subject, pertaining to contemporary life in Nevada, head for the excellent exhibit on neon lighting in Las Vegas. The exhibits are augmented by temporary displays of such items as Indian baskets, fiber arts, and saddle blankets. *700 Twin Lakes Drive • Map J1 • 702 486 5205 • Opening hours vary • Admission charge*

Chinatown Plaza

Casinos Beyond the Neon

Although for the past 30 years Las Vegas has been a sprawling city with shopping centers and clusters of businesses in the various neighborhoods, almost all of the hotel/casinos were concentrated in two areas – downtown and along the Strip. In the 1980s, when the city's population began its explosive growth, a number of neighborhood hotel/casinos were built. Visitors who venture beyond the neon for gaming may be pleasantly surprised to find a friendly atmosphere and lovely surroundings *(see p88).*

Ethel M. Chocolate Factory

Take a free tour to view the glass-enclosed, spotless, white kitchens where the diligent candy-makers concoct their sweet creations. Find out what the large stainless steel machines do, and admire the finished confections wrapped in their foil of emerald, ruby, sapphire, and other jewel colors. Every tour participant receives a free chocolate at the end of the tour. Outside the factory is a lovely cactus garden, with plants clearly identified. ◈ 1 Sunset Ray, Henderson • Map E5 • Open 8:30–7pm daily • Free

Ethel M. Chocolate Factory

Sunset Park

Las Vegas Speedway and Carroll Shelby Museum

Completed in 1996, the 107,000-seat Las Vegas Speedway was the first new super-speedway to be built in the southwest USA in more than two decades. The 1,500-acre facility has 24 different race tracks, food courts, a wedding chapel with racing-related stained glass windows, three levels of open-air grandstand viewing, a VIP party room, and luxury skybox suites. Important races staged here include the Winston West. A museum in the grounds is devoted to racing driver Carroll Shelby and his beautiful cars. ◈ 6755 Speedway Blvd • Map E1 • Museum tours at 10:30am daily

Masquerade Village Show in the Sky

The complex is designed to resemble an idyllic fishing village in northern Italy, complete with window boxes and balconies. The "Show in the Sky" consists of four lavish floats that travel on a track suspended above the village perimeter. Costumed performers toss beads and trinkets to the audience below. ◈ Rio Suite Hotel, 3700 W. Flamingo Rd; • Map C4 • 702 252 7777 • Hourly shows from 4–10pm • Admission charge to ride

Sunset Park

Undeniably the city's most popular park, Sunset offers

basketball, tennis, and jogging (*see p61*); a place to fly kites and sail boats; some of the best picnic spots in town; and a swimming pool. There's a dog run, too. ⊗ *2601 E. Sunset Rd • Map D5*

9 Marjorie Barrick Museum of Natural History

The museum centers around desert mammals, reptiles, and insects native to the southwest. It also contains exhibits focusing on the area's anthropology, archeology, and early-day architecture. ⊗ *UNLV campus • Map Q4 • Open 9am–5pm Mon–Fri, 10am–5pm Sat • Free*

10 Henderson Farmers Market

The market had its beginnings in 1999 and keeps getting bigger each season. Farmers drive from the California valleys to sell their produce year-round; in the summer season, they're joined by Nevada growers. No matter the season, artisans are on hand, selling everything from hand-painted china and rag dolls to house plants and inlaid chess sets. ⊗ *City Hall, Henderson • Map G6*

Two Excursions Beyond the Neon

Morning

⊙ Begin with an early morning stroll around the UNLV campus, stopping at the **Marjorie Barrick Museum of Natural History**.

Drive through the Green Valley area to **Foxcroft Park** (*see p85*) where if children are in your party, the play equipment will be the main attraction. Then it's on to the **Ethel M. Chocolate Factory** for the free tour and walk around the cactus garden.

If you can, include the **Henderson Farmers Market** in your itinerary. On the way back to your hotel, lunch at one of the terrace tables around the **interactive fountains at Green Valley Center** (*see p66*). You'll have the afternoon free or, if traffic is not too heavy, you can take a second excursion.

Afternoon

Begin at the **Nevada State Museum** (*see p85*). Motor-racing fans should then make their next stop the **Las Vegas Speedway**.

Finish up at **Chinatown Plaza** (*see p85*), where the herbalist-health food shop is a repository for remedies such as dried sea horses (good for the kidneys), herbs, and shark fins.

After an hour or two shopping, head up to the second floor of the Plaza, where you have a choice of different Asian restaurants for dining. Among them are Plum Tree Inn, Pho Vietnam Restaurant, Kapit Bahay Filipino Fast Food, and Dragon Sushi.

Left **Regent Las Vegas** Center **Sunset Station** Right **Texas Station**

TOP 10 Casinos

1 Rio
The Rio has more video poker machines than most, and a friendly feeling associated with casinos that rely on local trade for repeat business. *(See also p36.)* ✆ 3700 W. Flamingo Rd • Map C4 • 702 252 7777

2 Regent Las Vegas
A great place during daytime for people who want to gamble in a quiet, relaxing, upscale atmosphere. *(See also p36.)* ✆ 211 N. Rampart Blvd • Map A3 • 702 869 7777

3 Santa Fe
A mid-size gambling floor (1,700 slots), the Santa Fe is patronized primarily by locals and is one of the more pleasant casinos beyond the neon *(See also p36.)* ✆ 4949 N. Rancho Drive • Map A1 • 702 658 4900

4 Hyatt Regency Lake Las Vegas
The hands-down winner for surroundings, with sweeping views of the lake and mountains. *(See also p37.)* ✆ 101 Monte Lago Blvd, Henderson • Map H4 • 702 567 1234

5 Fiesta
From cocktail waitresses in jewel-toned satin outfits to the gaily patterned carpets on the floor, the casino evokes party time. *(See also p37.)* ✆ 2400 N. Rancho Drive • Map B2 • 702 631 7000

6 Texas Station
The theme is of a 19th-century town in the Lone Star state of Texas, with wagon wheels and gunpowder barrels. ✆ 2101 N. Rancho Drive • Map B2 • 702 631 1000

7 Sunset Station
Mediterranean-themed casino with wrought-iron balconies. Natural light makes it more pleasant than most. ✆ 1301 W. Sunset Rd, Henderson • Map F6 • 702 547 7777

8 Sam's Town
One of the largest non-Strip casinos with more than 3,300 slots, video poker, and keno machines. ✆ 5111 Boulder Hwy, Las Vegas • Map E4 • 702 456 7777

9 Orleans
There's a feeling of Mardi Gras in the casino, which is patterned after New Orleans' Vieux Carré. ✆ 4500 W. Tropicana Ave • Map B4 • 702 365 7111

10 Arizona Charlie's
Dude-ranch touches include deer antler chandeliers. Pai gow poker and Royal Match 21 are included in the games. ✆ 740 S. Decatur Blvd • Map B3 • 702 258 5200

For more hotels and casinos in Las Vegas **See pp32–7**

Price Categories

For a standard, double room per night (with breakfast if included), taxes, and extra charges.

$	under $50
$$	$50–$100
$$$	$100–$150
$$$$	$150–$200
$$$$$	over $200

Left **Polo Towers** Right **Rio All-Suite Hotel**

🔟 Hotels and Motels

1 Regent Las Vegas
Composed of two hotels, the Palms Tower Hotel and the Spa Tower Hotel, with great restaurants such as Gustave Mauler's Spiedini Ristorante. ◈ *221 N. Rampart Blvd • Map A3 • 702 869 7777 • $$$$*

2 Hyatt Regency Lake Las Vegas
The 496 guest rooms offer great views and all kinds of upscale facilities to round out the charms of this golfers' paradise. ◈ *101 Monte Lago Blvd, Henderson • Map H4 • 702 567 1234 • $$$$$*

3 Polo Towers
Condominium offering nightly rentals when the units are not occupied by time-share members. Great for families. ◈ *3475 Las Vegas Blvd S. • Map C4 • 702 261 1000 • $$$*

4 Rio All-Suite Hotel
Perfect for visitors who want the total resort experience without the congestion of the Strip. *(See also p33.)* ◈ *3700 W. Flamingo Ave • Map C4 • 800 752 9446 • $$$*

5 Marriott Hotel and Resort
Business people are among the hotel's most frequent customers. ◈ *325 Convention Center Drive • Map C3 • 702 650 2000 • $$$$*

6 Courtyard by Marriott
Popular with trade show attendees. Breakfasting away from the madding crowds is a real plus. ◈ *3275 Paradise Rd • Map C4 • 702 791 3600 • $$$$*

7 The Orleans
French Quarter-themed hotel, with green-shuttered windows and wrought-iron balconies. ◈ *4500 W. Tropicana Ave • Map B4 • 702 365 7111 • $$$$*

8 Sunset Station
Experience almost all the Las Vegas diversions in an away-from-the-Strip location: shopping at the Galleria *(see p52)*, golf, and casino action. ◈ *1301 W. Sunset Rd, Henderson • Map F6 • 702 547 7777 • $$$*

9 Emerald Springs Holiday Inn
The attractive 150-room motor hotel is a favorite with visitors who want to be near the bright lights without overdoing the gaming atmosphere. ◈ *325 E. Flamingo Rd • Map C4 • 702 732 9100 • $$*

10 Santa Fe
A hit with people who love vacations with active sports for its ice skating rink and 60-lane bowling alley. Golf packages are also available. ◈ *4949 N. Rancho Drive • Map A1 • 702 658 4900 • $$$*

Left **Wienerschnitzel** Center **Big Mama's** Right **Romano's Macaroni Grill**

TOP 10 Family Restaurants

1 Crocodile Café
Kid-friendly eatery at the Green Valley Center *(see p66)*, where your children will even get away with coloring their placemats. Youngsters love the meatloaf and soft tacos; grownups savor the red curry risotto with scallops. ⊗ *4500 E. Sunset Rd • Map E5 • $*

2 Hard Rock Café
Huge three-decker bacon, lettuce, and tomato sandwiches, great hamburgers, and chocolate chip cookie pie. ⊗ *4475 Paradise Rd • Map Q3 • 702 733 7625 • $*

3 Original Pancake House
The portions are huge; the pancakes, divine. And so many varieties – blueberry, apple, plate-size German pancakes, or buttermilk hotcakes as small as silver dollars. ⊗ *3460 E. Sunset Rd • Map E5 • $*

4 Toss Asian Cuisine
Ingredients are tossed, with marvelous results: *lo mein*, catfish in black bean sauce, *kung pao* shrimp. ⊗ *4500 E. Sunset Rd • Map E5 • 702 451 8677 • $$*

5 Wienerschnitzel
Drive-thru hotdog stand, with both the traditional pickles-with-mustard dogs and variations. ⊗ *4001 W. Sahara Ave (and other locations) • Map B3 • $*

6 Romano's Macaroni Grill
Bruschetta with a selection of toppings, fried mozzarella cheese, Italian *panini* sandwiches, and mouth-watering pasta. ⊗ *2400 W. Sahara • Map B3 • 702 248 9500 • $*

7 Souper Salad
Soups, muffins, and salads that are a real bargain, especially for families on Sundays when children eat free. ⊗ *2051 N. Rainbow Blvd • Map A2 • 702 631 2604 • $*

8 Big Mama's
Creole and Cajun dishes such as jambalaya, creole gumbo, okra, fish cakes, and sweet potato pie. ⊗ *2230 W. Bonanza Rd • Map D3 • 702 597 1616 • $$*

9 Jamm's on Rainbow Blvd
The place for breakfast: scrumptious french toast and eggs fixed to your liking. ⊗ *1029 S. Rainbow Blvd • Map A4 • 702 877 0749 • $$*

10 Hill Top House Supper Club
Seafood, chicken (try the pan-fried version), frog legs, and excellent salads. ⊗ *3500 N. Rancho Drive • Map A1 • 702 645 9904 • $$$*

For salad bars, buffets, and brunches **See pp48–9**

Price Categories

For a three course	$	under $20
meal for one with a	$$	$20–$30
half bottle of wine (or	$$$	$30–$45
equivalent meal), taxes	$$$$	$45–£60
and extra charges.	$$$$$	over $60

Left **Indoor Swap Meet** Right **The Attic**

🔟 Shopping

1 Chinatown Plaza
A shopping center that serves the needs of the city's sizeable Asian community as well as Asian-American tourists and visitors from around the world. At festival times *(see p58)*, counters are piled high with moon cakes and treats linked to special days. *(See also p85.)*

2 The Attic
The merchandise pays homage to fashions of the past, such as 1940s pillbox hats and rhinestone jewelry, 1960s tuxedos, and 1950s-style hot pants and sequined eyeglasses. 🔵 *1018 S. Main St • Map K3*

3 Sampler Shoppes Antiques & Collectibles Mall
Casino memorabilia and the largest array of antiques in Las Vegas. 🔵 *6115 W. Tropicana Ave • Map D4*

4 Belz Factory Outlet World
A truly fabulous place for any shoppers in your party who may have "champagne" tastes but "house-wine" wallets. *(See also p53.)* 🔵 *7400 Las Vegas Blvd S. • Map C6*

5 Fantastic Indoor Swap Meet
The Swap Meet is the American equivalent of the European flea market: vintage kitchen appliances, tire chains, home-baked bread, mismatched chairs, etc. 🔵 *Decatur Blvd at W. Oakey • Map B3 • Open weekends*

6 Cost Plus World Market
Import bazaar with handsome tableware, furniture, foodstuffs, and art objects from all corners of the world. 🔵 *3840 S. Maryland Parkway • Map D4*

7 Shepler's
Nevada cowboys buy their bolo ties, boots, sheepskin jackets, big belt buckles, and cowboy hats here. 🔵 *3035 E. Tropicana Ave • Map D5*

8 Sergio's Showgirl Wigs
The hairpieces are favored by top hairdressers for production shows and Hollywood films. 🔵 *900 Karen Ave • Map M4*

9 Bell, Book, & Candle
Talismans, crystal balls, tarot cards, and other soothsayers' tools. Witchcraft lessons, too. 🔵 *1425 E. Charleston Blvd • Map D3*

10 Thriller
Provocative swimwear, sexy shoes, and evening wear advertised as "tasteful and classy." 🔵 *855 E. Twain Ave • Map E4*

For more on shopping See pp 52–5, 83 & 116

Left **Hoover Dam** Center **Boulder City/Hoover Dam Museum** Right **Lake cruiser, Lake Mead**

Lake Mead, Hoover Dam, and Laughlin

THE HOOVER DAM, MOST ASSUREDLY, *changed the face of the American West. Not only did it enable the production of vast amounts of electrical energy and establish a reliable water source, but it also eliminated flooding, to help agriculture in California's lower valleys. The project's commercial by-products in Nevada – Lake Mead, Boulder City, and the resort community of Laughlin – have infused billions of dollars into the state's economy and provided recreational opportunities for hundreds of millions of visitors.*

Left **View from Hoover Dam Visitor Center** Right **Lake Mead**

🔟 Sights Around Lake Mead and Laughlin

1. Hoover Dam Tour
2. Boulder City Historic District
3. Boulder City/Hoover Dam Museum
4. Lake Mead National Recreation Area
5. Lake Mead Marinas and Beaches
6. Laughlin's Casino Row
7. Lake Mojave
8. Petroglyphs near Laughlin
9. Oatman, Arizona
10. Avi Resort and Casino

Hoover Dam Tour

1 Hoover Dam Tour

Guided tours take participants deep inside the gargantuan monolith for an in-depth exploration of the dam's history, purpose, and inner workings. The Bureau of Reclamation opened an impressive $125 million visitor center and parking lot in 1995. The three-level, circular center includes a rooftop overlook, a rotating theater, and a gallery. Here you can learn the fascinating story of the settlement of the lower Colorado River valley and find out about the amazing technology involved in the production and distribution of hydroelectric power. *(See also p10.)* ◈ *Visitor Center, Hoover Dam • Tour reservations 866 291 TOUR*

2 Boulder City Historic District

It's worth including Boulder City on a Hoover Dam trip to appreciate the scale of work involved – the city was built as a model community to house dam construction workers. The grandest buildings are the Bureau of Reclamation and the Bureau of Power and Light; the Municipal Building; and the Boulder Dam Hotel. Most of the construction, however, was focused on the two- and three-room houses for the workers. *(See also p11.)* ◈ *Information from Alan Bible Visitor Center • Hwy 93 at Lakeshore Rd • 702 293 8906*

3 Boulder City/ Hoover Dam Museum

Built in 1933, the Dutch Colonial-style Boulder Dam Hotel now houses the Boulder City/Hoover Dam Museum. Actor Boris Karloff and other Hollywood stars stayed in the hotel's glory days, and Crown Prince Olav and Princess Martha of Norway hosted a party here in 1939. The out-of-town hotel declined in the postwar rise of Las Vegas as a tourist mecca, but, since the mid-90s, a group of volunteers has set about rehabilitating it. The museum itself includes memorabilia from the 1930s. *(See also p11.)* ◈ *444 Hotel Plaza, Boulder City • Open 8:30am–4:30pm daily • Admission charge*

4 Lake Mead National Recreation Area

After the completion of the Hoover Dam in 1935, the waters of the Colorado River filled the deep canyons that once towered above the river to create a huge reservoir. This lake, with its 550 miles (880 km) of shoreline, is the centerpiece of Lake Mead National Recreation Area, a 1.5-million-acre (600,000-ha) tract of land. ◈ *Information from Alan Bible Visitor Center • Hwy 93 at Lakeshore Rd • 702 293 8906 • www.nps.gov/lame*

Boulder City Historic District

For more on the Hoover Dam **See pp10–11**

Casino Row, Laughlin

5 Lake Mead Marinas and Beaches

Along many miles of varied shoreline, Lake Mead's marinas and beaches range from delightful tiny coves to long stretches of sand. Popular beaches include Boulder Beach, Callville Bay, Echo Bay, and Overton Beach. These have recreational vehicle sites with full hookups, and supplies available at nearby stores. Boxcar and Icebox coves are favorites with houseboaters. Callville Bay and Lake Mead marinas are close to Hoover Dam, while Temple Bar marina serves the lake's southeast reaches.

6 Laughlin's Casino Row

The establishments lining Laughlin's South Casino Drive may not be as dazzling as those along the Las Vegas Strip, but they offer extremely good value. Getting around is easier than in Las Vegas: a riverside promenade connects most of the casinos, or you can take a bus or shuttle boat. Tours of the Colorado are also available. ⓢ *90 miles (145 km) S. of Las Vegas • www.enjoylaughlin.com*

7 Lake Mojave

The 67-mile (107-km) long lake extends from below Hoover Dam to two miles (3.5 km) north of Laughlin, and is only four miles (6.5 km) at its widest. A National Park Service Visitor Center at Katharine Landing, just north of Laughlin, offers free guided walks by park rangers. These lead through the desert to the petroglyphs at Grapevine Canyon. Houseboats and pontoon rentals, as well as fishing tackle, are available at Katharine Landing and Cottonwood Cove. Record-size striped bass have been caught in Lake Mojave. ⓢ *Part of Lake Mead National Recreation Area • www.nps.gov/lame • Admission fee to park*

8 Petroglyphs near Laughlin

Christmas Tree Pass and Grapevine Canyon, just west of Laughlin on Hwy 163, are the best places to see the fascinating petroglyphs that were incised into the sheer cliffs of the canyons by members of the early Patayan group.

Echo Bay, Lake Mead

The line drawings and symbols may have served as the road maps of their day, directing hunters and fishermen. National Park Service personnel have located more than 150 Patayan camp sites between Davis Dam and Willow Beach, which is 10 miles (16 km) from the base of Hoover Dam. ⊗ *Part of Lake Mead National Recreation Area • www.nps.gov/lame • Admission fee to park*

Petroglyph near Laughlin

9 Oatman, Arizona

A century ago, Oatman was a thriving gold mining center; today, visitors are taken back to the old days of the Wild West, with burros roaming the streets and staged gunfights in the middle of town. The Oatman Hotel was where honeymooners Clark Gable and Carole Lombard stayed in 1939. The town has been used as the location for a number of movies, including *How the West Was Won*. ⊗ *General information 520 768 6222*

10 Avi Resort and Casino

In 1995, the Fort Mojave Indian tribe opened Nevada's first Native American-owned casino and the only Native American-owned gaming business in the USA operated under state regulations. "Avi" means money or loose change. The resort is located in an area that the tribe intends to develop as a planned community. *(See also p97.)*

Two Days at the Dam and Laughlin

Day One

🕐 Begin with early morning coffee at Railroad Pass Casino on Hwy 93, an old-timer among gambling dens. Afterward, continue on Hwy 93 to the historic **Boulder City** and **Hoover Dam** *(see p93)* for the amazing tour.

Go back along Hwy 93 to the junction with Hwy 95 and turn south toward Laughlin. Stop at the **Nugget** in Searchlight *(see p96)* for lunch and the chance to visit a typical small-town Nevada casino.

For a more picturesque route, turn off 95 and head east on the dirt road through Christmas Tree Pass. Spend the remainder of the day in **Laughlin**, perhaps hunting for bargains at the 50-store Horizon Discount Outlet.

Overnight at **Harrah's** *(see p97)* or another hotel along the river, and be sure to take an evening stroll along the promenade.

Day Two

Early next morning, golfers can tee off at the 18-hole Emerald River Golf Course. Alternatively, the Riverview Golf Course is just across the river in Bullhead City, Arizona.

Later, head for **Oatman**, an old-time western town about a half-hour's drive southeast from Bullhead City. In the afternoon drive back north to **Lake Mojave**. Be sure to make time to see the mysterious **petroglyphs** at Grapevine Canyon, off Hwy 163, before returning to your hotel in Laughlin.

Around the Region – Lake Mead, Hoover Dam, and Laughlin

95

Price Categories

For a three course meal for one with a half bottle of wine (or equivalent meal), taxes and extra charges.

$	under $20
$$	$20–$30
$$$	$30–$45
$$$$	$45–£60
$$$$$	over $60

Left **Bob's All Family Restaurant** Right **Sidewalk Cafe**

TOP 10 Places to Eat

1 Bob's All Family Restaurant, Boulder City

The place to order home-made soup or chili and big slabs of pie. Decor is cozy, and the waitresses are small-town friendly. ◈ *761 Nevada Hwy • 702 293 1668 • $$*

2 5 & Diner, Boulder City

This is straight out of the 1950s, with a jukebox, lots of formica, sandwiches, malted milks, and other diner delights. ◈ *Highway 93 • $$*

3 Nugget Restaurant, Searchlight

Dominated by a mural of the *Searchlight*, an 1880s riverboat. The signature dish is a jumbo corn muffin with sausage, scrambled eggs, and gravy. ◈ *Highway 95 • 702 297 1201 • $$*

4 The Steak House, Laughlin

A perennial winner of *Casino Player Magazine's* best steak house award. It resembles a Victorian railroad parlor car with 19th-century-style gas lamps. ◈ *Ramada Express Hotel & Casino, 2121 S. Casino Drive • 702 298 6375 • $$$*

5 The Buffet, Laughlin

Platters come piled high with peeled shrimp, smoked salmon, blackened prime rib, and great cooked-to-order omelets. ◈ *Golden Nugget, 2300 S. Casino Drive • 702 298 7111 • $$$*

6 Fresh Market Square, Harrah's, Laughlin

Salads of all sorts (pasta, potato, slaws, and gelatin), carved meats, fresh fruit, and a gala array of desserts. ◈ *2900 S. Casino Drive • 702 298 4600 • $$*

7 Fruit Basket Buffet, Laughlin

Decorated with stylized citrus trees and baskets of fresh fruit. Crowd-pleasers include complimentary beer and wine and a make-your-own sundae bar. ◈ *Flamingo Hilton, 1900 S. Casino Drive • 702 298 5111 • $$*

8 Granny's Champagne Brunch, Laughlin

This Sunday-only affair bans anyone under 21 or dressed in shorts, thongs, tank tops, or T-shirts. Blueberry blintzes, lobster, caviar, crab legs, and wild rice often appear. ◈ *Pioneer Hotel, 2200 S. Casino Drive • 702 298 2442 • $$*

9 Cabo Grill, Laughlin

The fishing-themed decor complements the bourbon shrimp sauté, broiled salmon, snow crab legs, breaded oysters, and frog legs. ◈ *Harrah's, 2900 S. Casino Drive • 702 298 4600 • $$*

10 Sidewalk Café, Laughlin

Contemporary deli offering sandwiches, soups, salads, and pasta. ◈ *1650 S. Casino Drive • $*

Nugget, Searchlight

Around Town – Lake Mead, Hoover Dam, and Laughlin

Price Categories

For a standard, double room per night (with breakfast if included), taxes, and extra charges.	**$** under $50
	$$ $50–$100
	$$$ $100–$150
	$$$$ $150–$200
	$$$$$ over $200

Left **Harrah's, Laughlin** Right **Ramada Express Hotel and Casino**

Places to Stay and Casinos

1 Harrah's, Laughlin
Spanish-themed property with its own sand beach, a casino with windows looking out on the river, five restaurants, and an ambience that makes it one of Laughlin's most popular places to stay. ◈ 2900 S. Casino Drive • 800 447 8700 • $$

2 Golden Nugget Riverside, Laughlin
A tropical atrium with cascading waterfalls, palm trees, and 300 species of tropical plants sets this hotel apart. The casino, with its 24 Karat Slot Club, is more attractive than most. ◈ 2300 S. Casino Drive • 702 298 7111 • $$

3 Don Laughlin's Riverside Resort, Laughlin
A total destination resort. Unusual features include two classic auto showrooms and an antique slot machine display. There's also an RV park with full hook-ups. ◈ 1650 S. Casino Drive • 702 298 2535 • $$

4 Flamingo Hilton, Laughlin
The hotel features a large pool overlooking the river and Arizona hills, three lighted tennis courts, a wedding chapel, and Laughlin's largest tour boat, the Celebration. ◈ 1900 S. Casino Drive; 702-298-5111 • $$

5 Ramada Express Hotel and Casino, Laughlin
Advertised as "the premier destination for mature travelers." There's a Sunday flag-raising ceremony, a free multimedia show called On the Wings of Eagles, and a 1940s Museum of Memories. ◈ 2121 S. Casino Drive • 702 298 4200 • $$

6 Avi Resort and Casino, near Laughlin
Native American-owned resort (see p95) with a large, sandy, riverside beach, video arcade, swimming pool, live entertainment, and 29 spa suites. ◈ Aha Macav Parkway • 702 535 5555 • $$

7 Best Western Lighthouse Inn and Resort, Lake Mead
A 70-room motor hotel with views of the lake. ◈ 110 Ville Drive • 702 293 6444 • $$

8 El Rancho Boulder Motel, Boulder City
Spanish-style motel on the main street. Some rooms have kitchens. ◈ 725 Nevada Hwy • 702 293 1085 • $$

9 Overton Arm Campgrounds, Lake Mead
The campground offers showers, restrooms, and fuel. Reservations are not accepted. ◈ Close to the tip of the lake's northern arm • $$

10 Seven Crown Resorts, Lake Mead
Houseboats in various sizes and with excellent facilities can be rented here. All houseboaters have to bring on deck are food and clothing. ◈ Highway 167, Echo Bay • 702 293 3484 • $$

Left **Petroglyphs, Valley of Fire** Center **Death Valley** Right **Scotty's Castle, Death Valley**

Parks and Preserves

L ESS THAN AN HOUR from the man-made extravaganzas and simulations of the Strip are natural wonders so dramatic and thrilling that humans could not begin to replicate them. Many of these wonders are geological.
The closest is Red Rock Canyon (see pp24–5). Also nearby are Zion National Park, with its fantastic rock formations, and Death Valley – the hottest place in North America – whose floor lies 282 ft (85 m) below sea level, making it the lowest elevation in the western hemisphere. Most famous is undoubtedly Grand Canyon, whose dimensions are breathtaking. Each region has its distinct flora and fauna, with some species found nowhere else on Earth.

🔟 Sights of the Parks and Preserves

1. Petroglyph Canyon, Valley of Fire
2. Lost City Museum of Archeology, Overton
3. Kolob Reservoir Road, Zion National Park
4. Zion Canyon
5. Bright Angel Point, North Rim, Grand Canyon
6. Yavapai Observation Station, Grand Canyon
7. Watch Tower, Grand Canyon
8. Scotty's Castle, Death Valley
9. Aguereberry Point, Death Valley
10. Dante's View, Death Valley

Zion Lodge, Zion Canyon

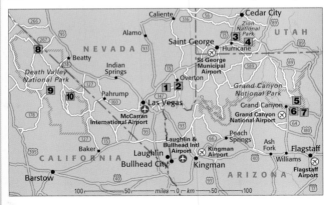

For more on the Grand Canyon See pp16–19

Left **Petroglyph Canyon** Right **Canyon Lodge, North Rim, Grand Canyon**

1 Petroglyph Canyon, Valley of Fire

Petroglyph Canyon is the Valley of Fire's most popular attraction, carrying as it does the park's largest concentration of petroglyphs – primarily symbols incised by prehistoric Native Americans from the Lost City *(see below)*. The purpose of the petroglyphs is unclear: some may have been no more than the road signs of their day, while others might have had a religious or mystical significance. Trail markers point out interesting sites along the way. ✆ *Map U2 • 702 397 2088 • Admission charge for park*

2 Lost City Museum of Archeology, Overton

Artifacts salvaged from Pueblo Grande de Nevada – now known as the Lost City – before it was inundated by Lake Mead are displayed at this pueblo-style museum. Exhibits include a reconstruction of the village, hunting weapons, and pottery. *(See also pp10–11.)* ✆ *721 S. Moapa Valley Blvd, Overton • Map U2 • Open 8:30am– 4:30pm daily • admission charge*

3 Kolob Reservoir Road, Zion National Park

Also called Kolob Terrace Road, this makes for a great scenic drive, taking in the multicolored Moenkopi Formation rocks, North Creek, Tabernacle Dome (a mass of red rock), cinder cones, canyons, valleys, and forests. ✆ *Map U1 • Information from Zion Canyon Visitor Center, Hwy 9, nr Springdale • 435 772 3256*

4 Zion Canyon

This makes for another splendid scenic drive, ending at the Temple of Sinawava. Of special interest is a mass of debris caused by a landslide 4,000 years ago. If you can stay, head for Zion Lodge *(see also p107)*, and, if you have no air-conditioning, gaze longingly at the shady groves of cottonwood, velvet ash, and box elder. Near the end of the drive is a turning that affords excellent views of the Great White Throne. ✆ *Map V1 • Information from Zion Canyon Visitor Center, Hwy 9, nr Springdale • 435 772 3256*

5 Bright Angel Point, North Rim, Grand Canyon

The North Rim of Grand Canyon may be more remote than the South Rim, but it is worth the effort. From Bright Angel Point (situated on an ancient trail) are spectacular canyon views. ✆ *Map V2 • North Rim Visitor Center, Bright Angel Peninsula • Open May–Oct*

View from the North Rim

 Following pages **Death Valley**

Left **Hopi House by Mary Colter, Grand Canyon** Right **Road to Mount Zion**

6 Yavapai Observation Station, South Rim, Grand Canyon

For a visual introduction to Grand Canyon geology, you can scarcely beat the view from Yavapai (also spelled Yavapai) Observation Station. Look down to the canyon floor for views of the Phantom Ranch lodge and the Colorado River. The river flows along the bottom of the canyon, no less than 5,000 ft (1,500 m) below the rim. From this great height it doesn't look very threatening, even with binoculars, but from the canyon floor it's a wildly impressive sight. ◈ *5 miles (8 km) N of south entrance • Map V2 • Open 8am–8pm*

7 The Watchtower, Desert View, Grand Canyon

A fanciful recreation of an Ancestral Pueblo, this landmark structure was designed by local architect Mary Colter in 1932. The upper floor of the stone-built tower is decorated with Hopi murals. A gift store and refreshments are available. Other Colter designs near by include Hopi House, Hermit's Rest, the Lookout Studio, and the cabins at Phantom Ranch lodge. ◈ *On Hwy 64 at Desert View • Map V2 • General infomation www.nps.gov/ deva • Free*

Ancient Rocks

The Grand Canyon reveals more of the earth's geological history than anywhere else on the planet (some of its rocks may be 1.7 billion years old). The mesas and cliffs of Zion National Park, too, were laid down and sculpted by the elements over millions of years. The youngster, Death Valley, has become visible only in relatively recent times: the lake that once filled it dried up a mere 10,000 years ago.

8 Scotty's Castle, Death Valley

Less of a castle than a Mediterranean-style mansion, the main man-made visitor attraction at Death Valley was built in the 1920s by the Chicago insurance magnate Albert Johnson. But Wild West show cowboy and conman Walter Scott had a habit of bragging that the spread was his, and it came to be called Scotty's Castle after him. A nice twist to the tale is that, in his

Dante's View, Death Valley

Kolob Reservoir Road

last years, Scott was befriended by Johnson and spent his last years at the coveted castle. Tours of the interior are available year round: fine craftsmanship is evident in the intricate wood carvings, wrought iron, and ornate tiling. It is also possible to take a self-guided tour of the grounds. ✎ *Hwy 267, at N. end of Death Valley • Map S1 • Grounds 7am–6pm daily, guided tours hourly 9am–5pm • Admission fee*

9 Aguereberry Point, Death Valley

High in the Panamint Mountains, the point offers panoramic views across most of Death Valley, taking in Furnace Creek, the snow-capped Sierra Nevada, Devil's Golf Course, and other landmarks. The point is accessible by mountain bike, but you'll need excellent bike-handling skills to make the climb; there is a 13-mile (21-km) loop ride for those who want to try it. ✎ *Map S2 • Information from Furnace Creek Visitor Center • 760 786 2331 • Open 8am–5pm*

10 Dante's View, Death Valley

On the crest of the Black Mountains, this is one of the most spectacular overlooks in Death Valley. It is approximately 5,475 ft (1,668 m) above the Badwater salt flats – the lowest point in Death Valley – and is a wonderful place for watching sunrise. The name was inspired by Dante's *Inferno*. ✎ *Dante's View Rd, 25 miles (40 km) S. of Furnace Creek • Map S2*

Three Trips from Vegas

Although it is possible to visit Zion, Grand Canyon, and Death Valley in one trip, it makes more sense geographically to return to Las Vegas in between each place, making three separate excursions.

The Road to Zion

🕐 For an overnight trip to remember, drive east on Highway 15 to the Valley of Fire turning. Spend an hour or two on the park's scenic drive, hiking through **Petroglyph Canyon** *(see p99)* to Mouse's Tank and visiting the **Lost City Museum of Archeology** *(see p99)*. Then, back on Highway 15, proceed to Mesquite for lunch, making sure you are within reach of one of Zion's many viewpoints by sunset: you will be richly rewarded. Overnight in the park or at Springdale.

Grand Canyon

Take Highway 93 to Kingman, then Highways 40 and 64 to the national park. It is possible to view much of the canyon's grandeur by driving along the rim routes, but the total canyon experience involves hiking or riding to the valley floor, spending the night, and perhaps river-rafting. For insights into Native American culture, visit one of the reservations along the rim.

Death Valley

Starting out from Las Vegas again, head north-west on Highway 95 to Beatty, turning off on Highway 374. You can see the major sights easily in a day and a half, but if you wish to hike or golf, you'll want to allocate more time to the trip.

 For more information on touring the region **See p109**

103

Left **Pinon trees** Center Left **Iguana** Center right **Sagebrush** Right **Desert tortoise**

🔟 Local Flora and Fauna

1 Pine Forests
Dense forests of scrubby piñon pine, stunted by poor, dry soil, grow 6,500 ft (2,000 m) above sea level in Grand Canyon (the canyon's highest elevation is 9,000 ft, or 2,750 m). Once every seven years they produce bumper crops of edible nuts.

2 Wildflowers
Grand Canyon wildflowers include asters, sunflowers, globemallow, and Indian paintbrush. At Zion, look out for columbine, penstemon, Indian paint-brush, and many varieties of sunflowers. Death Valley has fewer species, but Panamint daisies grow in profusion.

3 Sagebrush
The Nevada state flower is found up to 10,000 ft (3,000 m) above sea level and grows as tall as seven feet (2 m). The dense clusters of tiny yellow or cream flowers bloom in late summer.

4 Birds of Prey
Red-tailed hawks are the most common predatory birds in all three parks, but at the Grand Canyon look out for the king of the skies, the golden eagle.

5 Tortoises
Two isolated populations of desert tortoise, the Mojave and the Sonoran, are found respectively in southern Utah and in the Grand Canyon, Death Valley, and other parts of the southwest.

6 Lizards
In Zion eastern fence lizards are among 13 local species, while chuckwallas, short-horned, and collared lizards all inhabit the Grand Canyon. Most common in Death Valley is the banded lizard.

Golden Eagle

7 Mountain Lions
These shy creatures roam the Grand Canyon, Zion, and the mountains around Death Valley, helping to control the small mammal populations.

8 Deer
The unmistakable stiff-legged jump and large ears of the mule deer distinguish it through your binoculars from its graceful relative, the white-tail deer.

9 Snakes
Most species in the parks are harmless, but give rattlesnakes and sidewinders a wide berth.

10 Bears
Black bears are occasionally seen on the higher plateaus at Zion, but both they and grizzlies have long since disappeared from the Grand Canyon area, and no bears are known to live in the mountains surrounding Death Valley.

For desert precautions See p133

Left **Temple of Sinawava** Center **Panamint Mountains** Right **Great White Throne**

🔟 Natural Formations

1 Atlatl Rock, Valley of Fire
The most famous petroglyph here depicts an *atlatl*, a notched stick used to add speed and distance to a thrown spear. 🔊 *Map U2*

2 Elephant Rock, Valley of Fire
Accessible via a short trail from the eastern entrance, this strange sandstone formation resembles an elephant's head – albeit with an oversize trunk. 🔊 *Map U2*

3 Temple of Sinawava, Zion National Park
The so-called temple is, in fact, an awe-inspiring mass of red rock. The religious name echoes many others in the park. 🔊 *Map V1*

4 Great White Throne, Zion National Park
The sheer face of the Great White Throne, familiar to climbers worldwide, rises a staggering 2,200 ft (670 m) from the canyon floor, making it one of the world's tallest monoliths. 🔊 *Map V1*

5 Kolob Arch, Zion National Park
Kolob Arch is too inaccessible to permit accurate measurements of its bulk, but it is thought to be as much as 230 ft high and 310 ft wide (70 m x 95 m). 🔊 *Map V1*

6 Marble Canyon, Grand Canyon
The confluence of the Little Colorado and Colorado Rivers has carved out the great Marble Canyon (which is also a great place for trout fishing). 🔊 *Map V2*

7 Inner Gorge, Grand Canyon
Sheer granite cliffs drop 1,000 feet (300 m) to the canyon floor to form this vertiginous gorge. Two nerve-testing suspension bridges make the crossing near Phantom Ranch. 🔊 *Map V2*

8 San Francisco Mountains, Grand Canyon
Named the "Kingdom of St. Francis" by explorer Marcos de Nizo, the range rises to an impressive 12,655 ft (3,857 m). 🔊 *Map V2*

9 Funeral Mountains, Death Valley
A geological fault line was responsible for tilting these spectacular mountains on their sides. 🔊 *Map S1*

10 Panamint Mountains, Death Valley
The Panamints are honorary park members, lying as they do just outside it. Head for Aguereberry Point for amazing views of the Funeral Mountains and the Sierra Nevada beyond. 🔊 *Map S2*

Funeral Mountains

For more on the Grand Canyon **See pp16–19**

Price Categories

For a three course meal for one with a half bottle of wine (or equivalent meal), taxes and extra charges.	**$** under $20
	$$ $20–$30
	$$$ $30–$45
	$$$$ $45–£60
	$$$$$ over $60

Left **Thunderbird, Zion** Right **Flanigan's Café, Zion**

Places to Eat

1 El Tovar Dining Room, Grand Canyon

The room is built of pine logs and stone and features fine china, crystal, and linen-covered tables. Fresh seafood is flown in daily, and the veal dishes are excellent. ⊗ *El Tovar Hotel, South Rim • Map V2 • 303 297 2757 • $$$*

El Tovar Dining Room

2 Coronado Room, Grand Canyon

Prime rib, chicken marsala, and stuffed trout are favorites at this Spanish-style eatery.
⊗ *Best Western Squire Inn, Tusayan • Map V2 • 520 638 2681 • $$$*

3 Moqui Dining Room, Grand Canyon

Southwest American and Mexican food. ⊗ *Moqui Lodge • Map V2 • 303 297 2757 • Open Mar–Nov • $$$*

4 Arizona Steak House, Grand Canyon

A Southwest decor in muted pastels is the setting for the all-American favorite of big steaks, baked potatoes, and crisp salads. ⊗ *Grand Canyon Village • Map V2 • 303 297 2757 • $$$$*

5 Maswick Lodge Cafeteria, Grand Canyon

Wholesome food at reasonable prices. For a pre- or post-meal drink, the lodge includes a sports bar with wide-screen TV. ⊗ *Map V2 • Maswick Lodge • 303 297 2757 • $*

6 Flanigan's Café, Zion

Among the house specialties are salads, pasta, red trout, chicken, Utah lamb, and Black Angus beef. ⊗ *Springdale • Map U1 • 435 772 3244 • Open for dinner only • $$*

7 Kolob Canyon Picnic Area, Zion

Buy picnic provisions at Oscar's Deli and a bumbleberry pie at the Bumbleberry Restaurant in Springdale for an al fresco meal in grander surroundings than any restaurant. ⊗ *Map U1 • $*

8 Thunderbird Resort Dining Room, Zion

American fare in a family dining room, where the pies, breads, and sweet rolls are homemade. ⊗ *Mt Carmel Jtn • Map U1 • 435 648 2203 • $$*

9 The Inn Dining Room, Death Valley

Elegant dining room with lace tablecloths, firelight flickering on the adobe walls, and views of the Panamint Mountains. Continental fare is served in a six-course, prix fixe menu (try lamb chops as your entrée). ⊗ *Furnace Creek Inn • Map S1 • 760 786 2361• $$*

10 Stovepipe Wells Village, Death Valley

All-American fare, including an all-you-can-eat buffet in the summer. ⊗ *Stovepipe Wells • Map S2 • 760 786 2387 • $$*

Left **Best Western Zion Park Inn** Right **Furnace Creek Inn**

Price Categories

For a standard,	$	under $50
double room per	$$	$50–$100
night (with breakfast	$$$	$100–$150
if included), taxes,	$$$$	$150–$200
and extra charges.	$$$$$	over $200

TOP10 Places to Stay

1 Best Western Squire Inn, Grand Canyon

The 250-room inn has its own tennis court, heated pool, sauna, billiards, video games, beauty salon, and bowling alley. ◈ *Tusayan • Map V2 • 520 638 2681 • $$$*

2 El Tovar Hotel, Grand Canyon

Historic hotel built by pioneer resort builders, the Fred Harvey Company, in 1905. It is patterned after the great hunting lodges of Europe with a stone fireplace and mounted animals. ◈ *South Rim • Map V2 • 303 297 2757 • $$$*

3 Grand Canyon Lodge

The only hotel accommodation on the North Rim of the canyon, this lodge has cabins and a few modern motel rooms. Advance reservations are essential. ◈ *Bright Angel Point • Map V2 • 303 297 2757 • $*

4 Grand Canyon Trailer Village

With 250 RV hook-ups and 100 tent sites, this is one of the larger, privately run, year-round campgrounds. ◈ *Grand Canyon Village • Map V2 • 520 638 2887 • $*

5 Zion Lodge

The complex includes 40 cabins with gas log fireplaces and private porches, and 75 motel rooms, each with two queen-size beds. ◈ *Zion National Park • Map U1 • 435 772 3213 • $$*

6 Best Western Zion Park Inn

The inn is located at the foot of a 1,300-ft (430-m) cliff of Navajo sandstone. The 120 rooms are individually climate-controlled and some have kitchenettes. ◈ *1215 Zion Park Blvd, Springdale • Map U1 • 800 934 7275 • $$*

7 Cliffrose Lodge & Gardens, Zion

The setting is charming, with five acres of lawns, shade trees, and flower gardens along the Virgin River. Every room offers a spectacular view. ◈ *281 Zion Park Blvd, Springdale • Map U1 • 435 772 3234 • $$*

8 Furnace Creek Inn, Death Valley

Elegant and expensive, with glorious views of the Panamint Mountains. Guest rooms have quality furnishings. ◈ *Furnace Creek • Map S1 • 760 786 2361 • $$$$*

9 Furnace Creek Ranch, Death Valley

The rustic hostelry offers two spring-fed pools (the water is very warm), golf, tennis, and horseback riding. ◈ *Furnace Creek • Map S1 • 760 786 2361 • $*

10 Stovepipe Wells Village, Death Valley

A bit off the beaten track, this is not a fancy place but has a pool, saloon, and general store. The nearby sand dunes are a photographer's delight. ◈ *Stovepipe Wells • Map S2 • 760 786 2387 • $$*

Left **Hikers** Center left **Lake Mead marina** Center right **Sign on desert road**

TOP10 Hiking Trails

1 Mouse's Tank, Valley of Fire
"Mouse" was the name of a Native American outlaw. The moderately easy, self-guiding trail to Mouse's Tank (a series of natural catchments) passes the best petroglyphs in the park.

2 Canyon Overlook Trail, Zion National Park
A moderately difficult, short, day-hike to the overlook, which is right above the Great Arch.

3 Observation Point – Hidden Canyon Trail, Zion
The 7.5-mile (12-km) round-trip hike is moderately difficult to Hidden Canyon, then strenuous to Observation Point, but the view from the point is the park's finest.

4 Riverside Walk, Zion
The paved walk at the base of a gorge is especially delightful in early October when the fall foliage is at its most beautiful.

5 Bright Angel Trail, Grand Canyon
The entire 19-mile (30-km) round-trip descends 4,400 ft (1,450 m) and takes most hikers two days. Along the way are rest houses and a campground.

6 Rim Trail, Grand Canyon
Extending from the Village area, the partially paved trail can be accessed at many points between the West Rim and its terminus at Yavapai Point. There's little elevation change and spectacular views.

7 South Kaibab Trail, Grand Canyon
Access to the trailhead is by shuttle bus, which operates year-round. The trail is very steep and almost 12 miles (19 km) long.

8 Wildrose Canyon to Wildrose Peak, Death Valley
Climbs through woodlands to the crest of the Panamint Mountains.

9 Golden Canyon to Zabriskie Point, Death Valley
A low-elevation, six-mile (9.5-km) hike featuring the finest badlands scenery in the monument, and traversing an area of fully exposed rock strata that represents millions of years.

10 Coffin Peak Trail, Death Valley
This easy trail starts at Dante's View and follows a canyon into the Black Mountains. Upper reaches vegetation is dominated by mormon tea, shadscale, and spiny desert shrubs.

Kilns, Wildrose Canyon

For park visitor information See pp16–17, 99 & 102–103

Left **All-terrain vehicle** Center **Start of scenic route** Right **Mountain biker**

🔟 Commercial Tours

1 Las Vegas Tour and Travel
The Ultimate Freedom Tour begins with a flight over Hoover Dam and Lake Mead and continues to Grand Canyon. Participants then take a bus tour along historic Route 66 through Arizona. ✆ *702 739 8975*

2 Papillon Grand Canyon Helicopters
The adventure includes landing on the floor of the Grand Canyon. After exploration of Native American lands and a champagne picnic, the tour ends with views of Lake Mead, Hoover Dam, and the Las Vegas Strip. ✆ *702 736 7243*

3 Valley of Fire Adventures
Open-air jeep tours through the park's back country to view wildlife, plants, and formations. Lunch and hotel pick-up are included. ✆ *800 519 2243*

4 Grand Canyon Railway & Resort
These tours take clients by air from Las Vegas to northern Arizona where they board a vintage train on the Grand Canyon Railway and ride to the South Rim. A narrated motor bus tour, lunch, and return flight are part of the package.
✆ *800 843 8724*

5 Canyon Explorations
One of several companies providing hiking, interpretive trips, and whitewater rafting in the Grand Canyon. ✆ *520 774 4559*

6 ATV Wilderness Tours
Year-round guided trips in four-wheel all-terrain vehicles and jeeps. Three-hour to three-day outings are available. The company is based in St. George, Utah. ✆ *888 656 2887*

7 Adventure Photo Tours
First stop on this 10-hour tour is the ghost town of Grafton, where segments of the movie *Butch Cassidy and the Sundance Kid* were filmed. Then it's on to the east entrance, which is the most spectacular entry way into Zion National Park. ✆ *702 889 8687*

8 Nevada Tours and Travel
The "20-Mule-Team" Death Valley bus tour stops at Zabriskie Point, Badwater, China Ranch & Date Farm, and other points of interest. Lunch at the Furnace Creek Inn *(see p107)* is included. ✆ *702 650 5966*

9 L & E Las Vegas Tours
Death Valley day trips include sights such as the 120-ft (40-m) high sand dunes and the irregular salt flats called Devil's Golf Course. ✆ *702 453 5206*

10 Zion Ponderosa Ranch Resort
This is a resort that offers a number of guided activities, such as hiking, rappelling (abseiling), mountain biking, and horseback riding in Zion National Park. ✆ *435 648 2700*

Following pages **New York–New York Hotel, Las Vegas**

STREETSMART

LAS VEGAS TOP 10

Left **Golfing holiday** Right **Summer sun**

TOP 10 What to Pack and When to Go

1 Rate Changes
Hotel rates skyrocket when the weather is best – from about mid-March through May and September until the first part of November. However, days can be close to perfect during February, June, and November when rates are generally lower. If the weather doesn't figure heavily in your vacation plans, you'll be able to take advantage of lower prices, less traffic, and smaller crowds.

2 Tee-Timing
It's easier for golfers to get tee times during the winter months, March, and November. Although it can be windy, the temperature is usually comfortable for playing.

3 Consider Convention Dates
The three biggest annual conventions in Las Vegas, in November, April, and January, each attract well over 100,000 delegates. Do your utmost not to coincide with them: not only will room rates be at their highest, but traffic is heavy, and the lines waiting for restaurant service are daunting.

4 Daytime Wear
As far as clothes are concerned, just about anything goes. Although shorts and T-shirts are the uniform in very hot weather, you'll see people wearing everything from designer resort wear to jeans and leather jackets the rest of the year. Bathing attire should be reserved for swimming pool areas. Women wear cover-ups and men generally wear shirts and shorts over their bathing suits when going between their rooms and the pool. Upscale hotels provide robes for guests' use.

5 After Dark Apparel
While comfort generally rules the dress code, some moderately priced restaurants have signs saying "No shoes, no shirts, no service." Sport coats (casual-styled jackets) are required at some of the more expensive restaurants, but neckties are not always a requisite. Most people dress up when going to production shows or nightclubs; Las Vegas residents tend to dress more formally – and more flamboyantly – than visitors.

6 Health Matters
The sun shines an average of more than 300 days a year, so pack colored glasses, sunscreen, lip balm, moisturizer, and a hat.

7 Weather Wise
Keep in mind more than just the glorious sunshine: Las Vegas receives an average of only 4.21 inches of rainfall a year, with about half an inch falling during the wettest months, January and August. Humidity ranges from 14 percent to 41 percent. Winter is unpredictable: some days are very cold and windy, while others are warm enough for wearing shorts.

8 US Entry Requirements for Canadian Visitors
Canadians do not need passports, but must show a photo I.D., such as a citizenship card, when entering the USA.

9 US Entry Requirements for Overseas Visitors
Citizens from Australia, New Zealand, South Africa, the UK, and many other European countries can visit the USA for up to 90 days without a visa, so long as they have a valid passport. They will need to complete a Visa Waiver Form, usually on the incoming flight. Visitors from countries who do need a visa must apply to a US consulate or embassy, and may be asked for evidence of financial solvency and proof that they intend to return to their country of origin.

10 US Customs
Adult nonresidents are permitted to bring in a limited amount of duty-free goods. These include 0.2 gallons (1 liter) of alcohol, 200 cigarettes, 50 cigars (but not Cuban), and up to $100 worth of gifts. Cash amounts over $100,000 should be declared on entry.

For advice on health and things to avoid See pp131–3

Left **McCarran International Airport** Center **Car-rental agency** Right **Fly-drive option**

ᴛᴏᴘ10 Arriving in Las Vegas

1 Air News
If you're among the 43 percent of Las Vegas visitors who fly to McCarran International Airport, check out the airport website for information and maps. The eleventh busiest airport in the USA can be confusing when you don't know your way around.

2 Comparison Shopping
McCarran is served by all major US carriers and several international carriers, including Virgin Atlantic and British Airways, with both scheduled and charter flights. It's worth comparing prices thoroughly before making your reservation.

3 Fly-Drive and Gambling Deals
Fly-drive packages are a firm favorite with people on vacation in the USA. Investigate the so-called "Gamblers' Specials," too, which combine air travel and accommodation in Las Vegas.

4 Getting from the Airport to the City
The airport is 2.5 miles (4 km) south of the city center. Allow 10 minutes to travel by road between the airport and hotels on the Strip. Taxis, shuttles, and limousines wait outside the airport, and there are car rental agencies inside. The cheapest option is to take a bus: the CAT

(Citizens Area Transit) bus routes 108 and 109 run between the airport, downtown, and the Strip.

5 Paying Fares
If you have forgotten to bring enough change for transportation between the airport and your hotel, cash machines (ATMs) are located throughout the airport, and these accept standard cards such as Visa, MasterCard, and American Express, as well as other major US cards.

6 Car Rental
If you are renting a car from the airport, be advised that the rental price may not include three taxes, which total 21 percent, charged on all airport car rentals. If you are in a hurry, use one of the rental agencies with counters at the airport, but bear in mind that agencies with off-site counters generally charge lower rates.

7 Car Rental Documents
Visitors who plan to rent a car must remember to bring along a valid driver's license and major credit card, both of which are required by all agencies. Drivers must also be at least 25 years old to rent a car. If your own automobile insurance does not cover rental vehicles, it is wise to buy the rental companies' own coverage.

Directory

Air News
www.mccarran.com

8 Road Rules
Visitors from abroad who plan to rent automobiles would be well advised to familiarize themselves with basic US driving rules and signage before they begin driving. Information is available at most vehicle-rental agencies.

9 Arriving by Road
If you are driving to Las Vegas from another part of the USA, you'll probably access the city either via I-15, which goes from Los Angeles to Salt Lake City, Utah, and beyond, or via I-95, which connects Washington, Oregon, Nevada, and Arizona. Try to avoid peak traffic times on these roads: arrive before 4pm or after 7pm.

10 Arriving by Train
Just to get you used to the Las Vegas way of doing things, the Amtrak train station is located inside a hotel-casino in downtown Las Vegas *(see p81)*. If your luggage is light and you are staying downtown, you may be able to walk to your hotel from the station, but you will need to take a taxi or bus for destinations on the Strip.

For more on booking accommodations **See p135**

Left **CAT (Citizen Area Transit) bus** Center **Local taxi** Right **Monorail**

Getting Around

1 Foot Power
Walking may well be the best way to travel the three-mile-long Strip: the sidewalks are wide and the terrain is flat. Since the city covers a large area, however, and is crisscrossed by multi-lane streets, you'll need a car or public transportation when visiting attractions in outlying parts of the city.

2 Finding Your Routes
If you are going to be driving, procure a good map (the Rand McNally map, which can be obtained at supermarkets, drugstores, and booksellers, is excellent). The city is laid out on a grid, with only a few principal thoroughfares running obliquely.

3 Traffic Talk
In town, be prepared for fast driving and heavy traffic. Avoid driving during rush hours (about 7–9 am and 4–7pm). Congestion on the Strip begins in late morning and continues until after midnight, especially on weekends from mid-March through October and when large special events take place. The city's major streets are six to eight lanes wide.

4 Parking Lots and Garages
Hotel/casinos on the Strip and in Glitter Gulch provide free parking in high-rise garages. Elsewhere they have huge parking lots and/or garages. Almost all hotels offer valet parking. When valet parking is full, preference is given to hotel guests over casino visitors.

5 On-street Parking
When parking on the street, be sure to read all posted signs about parking restrictions to avoid incurring fines or having your car towed away. Fines for parking in disability-reserved spaces without a valid placard range from $100 to as much as $1,000.

6 Taxis
Hotel entrances on the Strip and downtown are the best places to find cabs. The standard fare is $2.20 for the first mile, $1.50 each additional mile, plus $0.35 a minute when stopped at a red light or stalled in traffic. In heavy traffic it can cost more than $20 to go from one end of the Strip to the other. Since taxi drivers know the city's less busy streets, a useful tip is to ask to be taken the quickest way rather than the shortest.

7 Trolleys, Trams, and Monorail
The exact fare of $1.50 is required for the Strip trolley (9:30am–2am daily), which stops at all major locations from the Stratosphere in the north to Mandalay Bay in the south. Free trams connect Treasure Island with the Mirage, Bellagio with Monte Carlo, and the Excalibur with Luxor and Mandalay Bay. A free monorail operates between MGM Grand and Bally's (9am–1am every day).

8 Public Transit System
The least expensive way to travel beyond downtown and the Strip is by CAT bus (Citizens Area Transit); CATs have an extensive network of routes. Fares are $2 on main tourist routes, $1.25 on others; seniors and children aged 5 to 17 pay ($1).

9 Hotel Shuttles
You may have to pay for the shuttle service between the airport and some hotels, but others offer a free service to shopping areas and sightseeing destinations.

10 Bike Riding
Bicycling along main arteries is not advised, but riding through residential neighborhoods and at Red Rock Canyon can be very pleasurable. Bikes can be rented from various outlets; fees usually include helmets and water bottles.

Left **Strip trolley bus** Right **Vegas-style private tour vehicles**

Sources of Information

1 General Information

For overall information about the city, including accommodations, attractions, and shopping, contact the Las Vegas Convention & Visitors Authority (LVCVA).

2 Business Information

Visitors interested in business in the area can contact the Las Vegas Chamber of Commerce, which will direct them to the appropriate sources.

Directory

Citizens Area Transit
702 228 7433

Las Vegas Convention & Visitors Authority
3150 Paradise Rd • 702 892 0711 • www.las vegas24hours.com

Las Vegas Chamber of Commerce
3720 Howard Hughes Pkwy • 702 735 1616

Asian Chamber of Commerce
900 Karen Ave • 702 293 2034

Black Chamber of Commerce
1048 W. Owens Ave • 702 648 6222

Latin Chamber of Commerce
829 S. 6th St, Suite 3 • 702 385 7367

Las Vegas Advisor
3687 S. Procyon Ave • 702 252 0655

3 Ethnic Affairs

Information about Las Vegas's various ethnic businesses and attractions is available from such organizations as the Asian Chamber of Commerce, Black Chamber of Commerce, and Latin Chamber of Commerce.

4 Organization Information

If you belong to a worldwide organization such as Rotary International or would like to meet people with similar vocational interests or hobbies, your best source of information is an Internet search engine such as www.google.com or www.yahoo.com.

5 Magazine Information

For insights into places and people who live in the Silver State, read *Nevada Magazine*, published by the Nevada Commission on Tourism. The magazine contains feature articles as well as information about attractions, special events, and entertainment.

6 Newspaper News

The *Las Vegas Review Journal* publishes dining and entertainment news throughout the week, as well as a "Best of Las Vegas" section once a year in March. You'll learn a lot by reading the ads, too!

7 Internet Info

For information on airlines, rental cars, and accommodations, use your favorite search engine to find websites with a Las Vegas focus. Among those you might find useful are www.visit lasvegas.com and www.lasvegas-nv.com.

8 Cost Cutting

Bargain hunters will save money by subscribing to the *Las Vegas Advisor*. This monthly newsletter, aimed primarily at people who like to gamble, includes accommodation and dining deals that are also of use to non-gamblers.

9 Tourist Stations

The tourist stations along the Strip not only sell commercial tours, but they also have display racks containing promotional material about various attractions, which may be of use to you.

10 Out-of-Town Source

People traveling to Las Vegas via I-15 south manage to find special offers and deals that don't seem to be advertised anywhere else: the tourist information center in Jean, Nevada (near the border with California) has a reputation for handling the best Las Vegas coupons.

Left **Bellagio's shopping arcade** Center **Belz Factory Outlet World** Right **Pawnshop**

🔟 Shopping Tips

1 Shopping Arcades
Count on finding the most interesting upscale shopping in hotel arcades such as Desert Passage at Aladdin *(see pp22–3)*, Bellagio's Via Bellagio *(see pp14–15)*, and Appian Way at Caesar's Palace *(see pp26–7)*. All these are on Las Vegas Boulevard South, otherwise known as the Strip.

2 Malls
You have several choices for major mall-hopping. Boulevard, Meadows, and the Galleria at Sunset *(see p52)* are patronized primarily by locals, while tourists from the majority at two upscale malls on the Strip – the Forum Shops at Caesar's *(see pp26–7)* and Fashion Show Mall *(see p52)*. The best sales at upscale shops such as Nieman Marcus and Saks Fifth Avenue (both at Fashion Show Mall) are held in January.

3 Bargain Buys
For bargains in high-quality merchandise, seek out the factory outlet centers. Belz Factory Outlet World *(see pp53 & 91)* is just a few minutes

south of the Strip, while Fashion Outlet Las Vegas is near the California border at Primm. It is especially worth visiting these stores at the end of summer, when the merchandise is marked down even further.

4 Antiques
The city's greatest concentration of antiques stores is on East Charleston Boulevard, two miles or so from downtown. If you have time to visit only one cluster of stores, go to Antique Square (2014-2026 E. Charleston Boulevard), where a dozen different shops make up the complex.

5 Ethnic Shops
For the best authentic ethnic shopping, go to the stores that serve Las Vegas's various ethnic populations such as Asian Market (935 E. Sahara), Supermercado del Pueblo #2 (4972 S. Maryland Parkway), India Sweets & Spices (953 E. Sahara Avenue), Nile Ethiopian Mart (860 E. Twain Avenue), and those in Chinatown Plaza *(see pp85 & 91)*.

6 Swap Meets
Swap meets, or flea markets, are usually held on Friday, Saturday, and Sunday, and are a great place to browse for bargains. The biggest meets are Fantastic

Indoor Swap Meet *(see p91)* and Broadacres Open Air Swap Meet (2960 Las Vegas Boulevard N.).

7 Pawn Shops
If you've never visited a pawn shop, Las Vegas is your chance. Much of the merchandise comes, of course, from gamblers in search of that little bit more money. The largest operation in town is Super-Pawn, with 12 outlets. A group of pawn shops are located in a street near Glitter Gulch *(see p80)*. If you want to make a purchase, don't agree to pay the first price you're quoted. Maybe not the second or third, either!

8 Business Hours
The larger malls and arcades are generally open 10am–9pm, seven days a week. Elsewhere stores may be closed on Sunday. Some of the Forum shops at Caesar's stay open until 11pm.

9 Taxes
Clark County levies a seven percent "sales and use" tax on most goods. This is added to purchases at the cash register.

🔟 Credit Cards
Most businesses accept Visa and Master-Card. American Express, Diners, and other cards are not accepted as widely; travelers' checks in US dollars are accepted at many stores.

Left Buffet restaurant **Center** The Convention Center **Right** Free tiger-watching at the Mirage

🔟 Ways to Save Money

1 Planning Ahead
Start planning early – the best airfares may require three months' advance purchase.

2 Airline Deals from Other Parts of the USA
Combined air and hotel packages from most US cities to Las Vegas are especially good bargains. Keep in mind that airline fares to hub cities served by a number of carriers are almost always less expensive than routes on which there are few competing airlines.

3 Airline Deals from Other Countries
When Las Vegas is among two or more destinations you plan to visit in the USA, price each segment of your trip's airfare separately. Visitors from Europe, for example, often save money by buying round-trip tickets from their home country to New York or Chicago and then traveling in the USA by using a combination of one-way bargain air tickets and rental cars.

4 Timing
Time your trip to save money. Hotel rates change from day to day, based on supply and demand. They're most expensive on weekends, holidays, and during big conventions and important events. The less restricted your travel dates, the more money you can save: a room that costs $200 a night on a busy May weekend can go for $50 in November. Airfares are usually lower during the winter months, too.

5 Car Rentals
Car-rental rates change even more rapidly – sometimes hourly. Since rental reservations don't require a credit-card guarantee, lock in a reservation when you're quoted a good price. You can always cancel it later if you find a better deal.

6 Freebie Sources
When you arrive in the city, go directly to the information center run by the Las Vegas Convention & Visitors Authority (see p115). Collect all the free magazines and brochures you can comfortably carry. Inside are coupons for special offers and money off shows and dinners, etc.

7 Meal Cost-Cutting
Eat your big meal of the day at noon. Lunch buffets usually cost a few dollars less than those offered at night, with virtually the same food served at both. If you're an early bird or a night owl, you'll save money on food: several casinos – notably those down-town and in outlying areas – offer low-cost meals between 11pm and 6 or 7am. These also work well for visitors affected by jet lag.

8 Discount Shopping
If you want to save money shopping, take one of the Strip buses to Vacation Village at the south end of the line. Transfer to the free shuttle that goes to Belz Factory Outlet World (see pp53 & 91). The bus will cost a couple of dollars each way.

9 Entertainment Savings
The extravagant nightly light and sound shows and street performances at the Fremont Street Experience (see p79) are all free. Many of the big hotels along the Strip put on spectacular free shows to entice people in (see p76). There are also less well-publicized free attractions such as the tropical bird display at the Tropicana Hotel and Casino. People-watching is entertaining, too (see p77).

10 Free Special Events
Every so often, casinos put on promotions, bands present concerts, and organizations sponsor other free events. These are listed in the calendar sections of local papers and the various free entertainment magazines.

For more on free or low-cost entertainment **See pp76 & 82**

Left **Lord of the Dance** Center **EFX** Right **The Dream King**

Types of Entertainment

1 Production Shows
Plan to see at least one production show (long-running show with spectacular production effects) while you're in town. A Las Vegas visit simply isn't complete without experiencing the excitement and professionalism of these top-notch performances. Although shows such as "O" and Siegfied and Roy are expensive, others that cost less than half of their prices are also very well done.

2 Showtime
Most big shows go on twice nightly, with one or two nights off a week (varying from show to show). Daytime shows usually cost less.

3 Dining Options
Although the trend is toward shows that don't include meals or cocktails (there are refreshment stands outside most theaters), some hotels feature dinner and cocktail shows. If you can, opt for the cocktail shows: they're less expensive. Moreover, the food at dinner shows doesn't tend to get rave reviews.

4 Other Shows
The production spectaculars aren't the only shows in town. Other long-running shows in hotel/casino theaters star magicians, comedians, and impersonators. Comedians on their way up also appear on Las Vegas comedy club stages.

5 Headliner Shows
If you're determined to see a particular entertainer perform in one of the city's famous headliner extravaganzas, order your tickets as soon as you hear about the performance. If you hesitate, you will probably still be able to buy tickets, but they will most likely be for the poorest seats in the priciest category. Las Vegas is a venue where top entertainers typically present just one performance; while the least expensive tickets may cost less than $100, top tickets can cost more than $1,000.

6 Lounge Shows
To stretch your entertainment dollars, take in a lounge show or two. You can watch some lounge acts for the price of a drink. Others are free.

7 Future Stars
If you like to know about the newest, most potentially hot acts, then go to see lots of lounge shows. Many of America's most celebrated entertainers – including Elvis Presley – appeared in Las Vegas casino lounges on their way to the top.

8 Chance Entertainment
In a town where entertainment is the name of the game, most Las Vegas visitors happen upon some unexpected treat during their visit. It may be a Dixieland band playing in a hotel plaza, a dance recital at a shopping center, a string quartet playing in a park, or strolling entertainers at the theme hotels.

9 Adults Only
Several clubs in the area around West Sahara Street south of downtown present adult-only entertainment. With names like Crazy Horse Saloon, Lacy's, and Palomino Club, they feature topless waitresses, amateur strip contests, and "beautiful friendly hostess dancers".

10 Culture
High culture doesn't necessarily come to mind when one thinks of Las Vegas. It is, in fact, the city's best-kept entertainment secret. Top-drawer artists from around the world perfom regularly here: Luciano Pavarotti has sung at the Mandalay Bay; top orchestras and ballet troupes can be seen at the university. In addition, performers in the Las Vegas shows take part in actors equity, ballet, and musical productions when not in their regular roles.

For more about shows and entertainment See pp38–43

Left **Illusionists** *Siegfried and Roy* Center **Lavish production at MGM** Right **Tommy Tune in** *EFX*

10 Tips on Buying Tickets

1 Advance Bookings

To avoid disappointment, order tickets for any production shows you want to see well in advance. You can do this either through your travel agent, by contacting the box office directly (when the production is at a hotel/casino theater, you can phone the hotel and your call will be transferred), or through a ticket agency such as Ticketmaster. It is almost impossible for ordinary tourists to buy tickets to the top shows such as "*O*" and *Mystère* on the day of the performance even if they are staying in the hotel where the show is playing.

2 Discount Outlets

In cities such as New York, San Francisco, or London, surplus same-day tickets for shows are sold at a discount at a central ticket outlet; this is not the case, however, in Las Vegas.

3 Standby

When you want to see a show and can't get tickets in advance, you will increase your chances of getting standby seats by arriving early so you get one of the first places in line.

4 VIPs

If you're a high roller, you probably won't have to worry about standing in line at shows or anywhere else. Just let the VIP desk know what you would like to see.

5 Charting Your Course

When it is possible, ask to see the theater's seating chart. It's probably true that in the new theaters there isn't a bad seat in the house. Still, some seats are better than others, and as long as they all cost the same price, it is worthwhile choosing the ones you want.

6 Tipping

Tipping the *maître d'* or usher isn't always necessary. A growing number of theater tickets are issued electronically, and your seat is determined before you enter the theater. At theaters that have table-seating, however, guests are seated at the maître d's discretion. Palming him a $20 bill will usually get better seats, but do it in a discreet way.

7 University Venue Tickets

Tickets for performances at the Judy Bayley Theater or Artemis Hamm Concert Hall on the university campus can both be secured from the same box office; consult the Las Vegas Convention & Visitors Authority or local press for contact details.

8 Other Cultural Venues

Tickets for cultural programs presented at such venues as community arts centers and outdoor amphitheaters are usually, but not always, available from commercial ticket agencies including Ticketmaster. The yellow pages of the Las Vegas telephone directory list the numbers of various concert venue ticket offices.

9 Tour Group Tickets

People who are interested primarily in seeing Las Vegas shows should consult with their travel agents about tours that include them in their itineraries.

10 Ticket Information

If you have a problem finding ticket sources, try contacting the Las Vegas Convention & Visitors Authority (see p115). Another good resource is the newsroom of the city's major newspapers.

Directory

Ticketmaster
702 474 4000

Left **Getting married at Bellagio** Center **Wedding chapel** Right **Elvis Presley's Vegas wedding**

TOP 10 Getting Married in Las Vegas

1 Getting a License
Marriage license requirements in Nevada have traditionally been less stringent than those in other parts of the USA. No blood tests are needed, nor is it necessary, after the license has been issued, to wait a set period before getting married. To obtain a marriage license, both partners must appear at the County Clerk's office in the Clark County Courthouse. Well over 100,000 weddings are performed in Clark County each year.

2 Identity Proof
Be prepared to produce proof of identity such as a driver's license, certified copy of birth certificate, passport, or military ID. Applicants who have been divorced must present evidence that their divorces have been finalized, including date, city, and state where the decree was granted.

3 Age of Consent
People aged 18 years and older do not need consent to get married, but those aged between 16 and 18 must either have a consenting parent present or else produce a notorized document from a parent giving his or her consent.

4 Time-Saver
Couples planning a St Valentine's Day or New Year's Eve wedding should get their licenses well in advance to avoid long lines at the County Clerk's office.

5 Wedding Officiants
Nevada law requires that couples be married by civil marriage commissioners, justices of the peace, or bona fide ministers.

6 Civil Ceremonies
Civil marriages are performed one block from the Courthouse in the office of the Commissioner of Civil Marriages, for a fee of $35. One witness is required in addition to the person performing the ceremony.

7 Religious Rules
If your decision to have a religious wedding in Las Vegas is not a spur of the moment one, then have your usual minister, priest, or rabbi contact the head of the church or synagogue in Las Vegas where you want the ceremony to be held. That way you can resolve any discrepancies that may exist between different denominations regarding preparation for marriage, publication of banns, and the like.

8 Prices
You need $35 – in cash – for the license. Budget $75 for the use of a wedding chapel in a no-frills ceremony, $50 for the minister, plus any flowers, music, or costume rental. Weddings featuring an Elvis impersonator as minister start at $150. Make arrangements for a wedding-chapel ceremony in advance: they can't oblige drop-ins when fully booked.

9 Venues
With more than four dozen chapels, hundreds of churches, synagogues, public parks, ballrooms, and scenic spots, the number of wedding venues is limited only by the imagination; some officiants may be unwilling to perform skydiving or helicopter ceremonies!

10 Same-Sex Ceremonies
Same-sex marriages are not recognized in Nevada, but there are Las Vegas wedding chapels, including the Gay Chapel of Las Vegas, that perform commitment ceremonies.

Directory

Clark County Courthouse
200 S. 3rd St • Open 8am–midnight Mon–Thu, & from 8am Fri around the clock to midnight on Sun, also 24 hours a day on all Nevada state holidays

Commissioner of Civil Marriages
309 S. 3rd St • Same hours as above

Gay Chapel of Las Vegas
1205 Las Vegas Blvd S. • 800 574 4450

Left **Little Church of the West** Center **Wedding chapel** Right **Romantic Pamplemousse**

TOP10 Honeymoon Packages

1 Hotel Packages

Since honeymoon packages are offered by virtually all of the hotels in Las Vegas, it definitely pays to shop around. The basic packages usually include an upgraded room, a bottle of champagne with souvenir champagne flutes, optional breakfast in bed, and dinner at one of the hotel's restaurants.

2 Seasonal Price Variations

Whereas wedding licenses cost $35 year-round and chapel fees remain fairly constant (St Valentine's Day and New Year's Eve being exceptions), honeymoon package prices are affected by the dates you choose. For example, a week-long honeymoon during the annual giant Comdex convention, with its 225,000 delegates, may well cost two to four times what it might during the preceeding or following week.

3 Bed-and-Breakfast Packages

If you fancy getting away from the crowds and bright lights, investigate bed-and-breakfast honeymoon packages and houseboat rentals (see also page 134).

4 Internet Deals

Explore your options on the Internet. Each major hotel has a web-site, as do many of the smaller ones. Most of these include information on package deals.

5 Do-It-Yourself

You may feel that rather than opt for a lavish package you can make your honeymoon more special by doing it yourself, finding a regular hotel package and adding your own romantic touches – a box of Ethel M. gourmet chocolates (produced in Las Vegas), dining at an intimate restaurant such as Pamplemousse (see p46) and seeing the shows you choose.

6 Accommodation Advice

As far as accommodations are concerned, the general rule is that the further away you are from the Strip, the less expensive the rooms. There are, however, two deluxe exceptions to the rule – the posh Regent Las Vegas at Summerlin and the exceedingly romantic Hyatt Regency at Lake Las Vegas (see p37).

7 Professional Planning

Las Vegas Weddings has been arranging weddings and honeymoons in the city since 1973.

8 Trousseau Tip

Save some of your trousseau money for lingerie shopping in Las Vegas. The little nothings sold at places like Bare Essentials and A Slightly Sinful Adventure are definitely unusual!

9 Wedding Photos

For an inexpensive souvenir of your honeymoon, have your picture taken in costume at the photo concession on the second level of Excalibur, or else have your faces photographed on a magazine cover at Cashman Photo in Desert Passage.

10 Films

Honeymooners keen on the movies might find it fun to rent a copy of the 1991 Nicholas Cage comedy *Honeymoon in Vegas*, which is set in the city, to watch on the VCR in their honeymoon suite.

Left **Sunset Station Casino sign** Center **Coin bucket** Right **Banks of slot machines**

Slot Clubs

1 Join Up
If you're planning to gamble, join a slot club. Almost every casino has one, which anyone over the age of 21 can join for free. These clubs give players various rewards in relation to the amount of gambling they do, whether they win or lose.

2 Maximizing Benefits
Compare clubs to determine which one has the prizes you like best and the most advantageous point system. For example, while the number of points required for similar rewards may be the same at two clubs, one of them may award two points for every five dollars that goes through a machine while the other requires only one dollar. You can join as many clubs as you like, but experts advise that you join only one so that you accumulate enough points to earn rewards.

3 Playing Cards
Insert your plastic membership card (issued upon registration) to get your points registered. When accumulated, these points can be exchanged for meals and discounts on rooms (or even free rooms), as well as logo items such as mugs, T-shirts, athletic bags, warm-up jackets, and caps. Some casinos offer cash rewards, too.

4 Slot-club Hosts
Almost every casino employs "slot-club hosts," who circulate around the casino. If you have questions about how to play various machines, ask them; ask, too, how long you have to play the machines to be "comped" for lunch, dinner, or entertainment in the casino's showroom (theater). This is accepted procedure, so don't be shy about asking.

5 Sign-up Savvy
Couples who are in Las Vegas for one trip should sign up together, since they will be issued two cards with points accumulated on the same account. Those who plan more trips to the area, however, will profit by signing up singly: casinos send offers such as a certain number of nights at reduced room rates; by signing up as individuals, the couple may be able to take advantage of twice as many nights at the reduced rate.

6 Payouts
Choose machines with the best payout schedules. These schedules are found on the front of each machine and indicate winning combinations and the number of coins paid out when a combination is hit. As experienced

machine players are aware, the video poker and slot machines in any given casino have varying payouts as well as payback ratios (the average percentage the machine pays back to the player).

7 Slot Club Money Management
Remember that in every casino game the house has the advantage (even the 100% and better return on the best-paying video poker machines is predicated upon perfect play). Losing $50 to earn a $6.95 buffet award is not a bargain.

8 Table Games
Many casinos include table games in their slot clubs. If you play table games at one of them, contact the pit boss to be sure your playing is included in the point count.

9 Cash-in Advice
Keep an eye on your watch when you plan to redeem your points. Many slot club booths close before midnight and don't open again until the next morning.

10 Future Plans
If you plan to return to Las Vegas quite soon, you might consider subscribing to the *Las Vegas Advisor*, which includes a monthly "Slot Club Update" column.

Left **Casino membership card** Right **Blackjack table**

Gaming Tournaments

1 Tournament Schedules

Gamblers should contact various casinos to determine if any gaming tournaments are planned for the time they will be in Las Vegas. These tournaments range from daily free events and those with low entry fees to four-day tournaments. Blackjack, slot machine, and video poker tourneys are the most popular.

2 Multi-Day Tournaments

Count on a good deal of free time during four-day tournaments, since actual play takes up only two or three hours. Entry fees usually include lodging (or rooms at reduced rates), some meals or food, and beverage credits for the entrant and a guest. Although entry fees may run into the thousands of dollars, typically they're in the $199 to $599 range. Prize money in the high-stakes tournaments can go as high as a million dollars.

3 Between Rounds

Keep in mind that the casinos' primary reason for putting on tournaments is their belief that participants will gamble in the casino during the time when they're not competing. Most regular slot or video-poker tournaments consist of three rounds of 20–30

minutes each at metered machines and require no money to be spent during tournament play. Winners of each round, as well as the players whose aggregate scores for the three rounds are highest, are awarded prizes.

4 Prizes

The amount of prize money varies, but the majority of tournaments award cash to a large percentage – perhaps a quarter – of the entrants.

5 Blackjack

If blackjack's your game, you'll find that tournaments generally consist of three rounds, with round winners advancing to semi-finals and finals. The entry fee usually covers a certain number of tourney chips, issued at the beginning of the tournament and again before the semi-final and final rounds.

6 High Rollers

If you're a high roller, be sure to get on the invitation list at your casinos of choice. Several casinos don't publicize their tournaments, but instead invite high-end players whose names have been selected from their databases. Complementary accommodations, food, and beverages are generally the properties' finest, and entry fees range all

the way from zero to thousands of dollars.

7 Tourney Money Management

For people with finite resources, it is more practical to play in tournaments that have entry fees than those with no fee but participants play with their own money. At tournaments with unlimited buy-ins, players may pay additional money to buy more chips or machine play as the tournament progresses.

8 Playing Plus

When you're competing in a gaming tournament that depends on a combination of luck and skill, stay ahead of the game by sticking to soft drinks and bottled water, rather than complementary alcoholic drinks.

9 Tournament Machines

Don't expect the machines on the casino floor to hit winning combinations as often as the tournament machines. High scores and frequent jackpots create excitement, so as a rule the machines used in tournament play are set to produce lots of action.

10 Repeat Invitations

If you enjoy the gaming tournament experience and want to be invited again, send a thank-you note to the casino's special events director.

Left **Croupier setting a roulette table** Center **Baccarat** Right **Keno**

🔟 Gambling Tips

9 First and Foremost

Remember: gambling is a business. The house almost always wins. Think of it as an evening's entertainment, not as a way of making money. Decide in advance what you are willing to spend, and quit as soon as you have spent it. If you do win anything but want to keep playing then cash in frequently (put your original stake, plus part of your profit, aside) to come out ahead.

1 Casino Games

Blackjack (which is also called "21") is the table game at which players have the best odds. Other popular table games include craps (dice), baccarat, roulette, poker, and three games based on Five Card Stud poker: Caribbean Stud Poker, Let 'er Ride, and Pai Gow.

2 Slot Machines

Many experts believe that slot machines (slots) are addictive. They're the big money-earners for Nevada casinos. Some – video poker, particularly – involve an element of skill. Others are purely games of chance. Newer machines incorporate elements that make them more enticing than the traditional slots.

3 Money Matters

Inserting $10 or $20 bills into slot machine receptors – instead of playing coins one at a time – allows for more rapid play, since players need only push a button and the selected amount of coins is deducted. When winning combinations are hit, payouts are added to the total rather than being ejected from the machine.

4 Reading the Payout Tables

Many people who are new to slot machines don't realize that you aren't able to win the highest jackpots posted on a machine unless you insert the maximum number of coins the machine will accept. This means you have to decide whether you want to risk larger amounts, or would prefer to be disappointed if you hit the big one and don't have enough coins in to collect it.

5 Keno

Odds of winning at keno are the lowest of all casino games. The game is based on selecting certain numbers (from 1 to 80) that you hope will be among the 20 numbered ping-pong balls ejected from a hopper during each game. Payouts are based on the number of "catches" (matching numbers selected). Most casinos have keno lounges.

6 Gaming Terms

It is helpful to know at least some of the casino jargon. Hand pay: winnings paid by casino workers rather than machines. Stickman: a casino worker who uses a hook-shaped stick to move dice around a craps table. Shooter: the player whose turn it is to roll the dice. Tokes: tips given for services rendered. RFB comp: complimentary room, food, and beverages (usually given to customers who spend a lot). High roller: someone who wagers large amounts. Bust hand: in blackjack, a hand that totals more than 21.

7 Gaming Chips

Remember when gambling at the tables that chips are not "play money." At all Las Vegas casinos, $5 chips are red, $25 chips are green and $100 chips are black. The colors of higher denomination chips may vary.

8 Coupon Caution

Take advantage of casino two-for-one or other coupons only if you plan to gamble anyway. Don't let them take advantage of you by enticing you into gambling.

10 Hand Pays

When you hit a jackpot that is paid by casino personnel rather than the machine, it is customary to tip. Any amount is appreciated, but most people tip from three to five percent; big spenders may go as high as 10.

Left **Laying bets during a craps game** Center **Craps dice** Right **Arizona Charlie's casino**

🔟 Gambling Risks

1 Forgetting to Take a Break

Don't gamble nonstop. Gambling can be mentally and physically exhausting. If you spend more than an hour deciding whether to hold 'em or fold 'em, or two hours hunched over a slot machine, gamblers' fatigue is bound to set in. Taking a break – perhaps a short stroll outside – will go a long way toward making you feel refreshed.

2 The "It's Due to Hit" Myth

Some gamblers have the idea that since a slot machine hasn't paid any jackpots for a long time, it's due. Not true. Each spin of the reels is an independent event and has nothing to do with what has gone before or will come after.

3 No Good at Math

Beware of nickel multiple-coin machines. Casinos make more profit on these machines than on any others. Most of them have nine pay lines, which means that nine coins must be played if you want to gamble on all the possibilities. How this translates in practice is that playing the maximum number of coins on all lines amounts to $4.50 each time you push the button.

4 Not Keeping it to Yourself

Don't boast about your winnings anyplace where strangers might hear you. You never know who they might be – con artists or worse.

5 Free Drinks

Resist the cocktail waitresses who circulate throughout the casinos frequently passing out free drinks to gamblers. People who drink excessively don't play as well as they might and have even been know to leave buckets of coins behind them when they go.

6 Air Pollution

If you don't like smoking, don't put up with smoke-filled rooms. Some casinos (usually the newer ones) have more effective mechanisms than others for getting rid of smoke. With so many casinos in the city, it isn't hard to find one of them.

7 Cashing Your Paycheck

All sorts of inducements – free drinks, free pulls on slot-machine handles, chances to enter drawings (prize draws) for cars and even houses – are offered so that people will cash their paychecks at casinos. Why? Because once a paycheck is cashed, it's easier to spend.

8 Neglecting to Set Yourself Limits

Don't neglect to set limits on the amount of money you can afford to lose. Conversely, it's not a good idea to set goals on how much you are going to win before you quit. Probabilities are that it will cost more than the goal itself to reach the goal. It's true that some people do win – at times enormous amounts. But the multi-million and billion-dollar hotel/casinos provide vivid proof that more money is lost than won.

9 Bad Deals

Resist the come-ons some casinos offer of $40 or even $100 in slot play for $20. Play is allowed only on specific machines, and it's only after paying their money that "suckers" learn the real rules.

10 Under-Age Gambling

Don't gamble unless you are 21 years or older. If apprehended, minors are either arrested or given a citation. In either case a court appearance will be required, as the offense is a misdemeanor and subject to penalties that can range from fines to community service or even jail sentences of up to one year.

Left **Lady Luck** Center **Learning the ropes** Right **Palace Station**

🔟 Gaming Lessons

1 Player's Anxiety
To overcome new-player jitters, it's wise to take lessons in the games you want to play. These are usually available at the casinos listed Monday through Friday: they last about an hour and are free.

2 House Rules
Even if you play poker or baccarat regularly with friends, the benefit of lessons is that you will learn the procedures and protocols of casino play. Not knowing the rules can be embarrassing.

3 Timing
You'll get more out of gaming lessons if you take them in the morning. Casinos – the setting for most lessons – tend to be much noisier and distracting as the day wears on, which can make it difficult to concentrate on what the instructor is saying.

4 Tipping
Although there is no charge for the classes, your instructor will appreciate a tip. Any amount between $2 and $5 would be appropriate.

MGM Grand

5 A Winner
For years the Riviera has offered probably the best gaming instruction program on the Strip. The lessons – which include craps, blackjack, roulette, baccarat for beginners, and poker – are held three days a week in the main casino.

6 Exotic Games
When you're ready to tackle Pai Gow, Caribbean Stud, and Let it Ride poker, phone Aladdin or New York–New York for their lesson times.

7 Downtown Lessons
If you want to keep away from the Strip, then Lady Luck is one of the few downtown casinos that offers gaming lessons.

8 Off-Strip Instruction
Further afield – and a good choice if you have a car and don't want any parking hassles – Palace Station Hotel and Casino is reputed to have good gaming instruction.

9 Classes in Japanese
Most gaming lessons are conducted in English. San Remo Las Vegas Casino, however, also offers classes to Japanese visitors. Go between 4:30pm and 11:30pm for instruction. Each participant gets a free deck of cards.

🔟 A Cautionary Note
So you've taken lessons. That doesn't mean you're an expert yet! Watch actual play before you start wagering, and then bet minimum amounts until you're experienced at casino play.

Blackjack

Directory of Casinos Offering Gaming Lessons

The Riviera
2901 Las Vegas Blvd S.
• 702 734 5110

Aladdin
3667 Las Vegas Blvd S.
• 702 736 0111

New York–New York
3790 Las Vegas Blvd S.
• 702 740 6969

Lady Luck
206 N. 3rd St
• 702 477 3000

Palace Station
2411 W. Sahara Ave
• 702 367 2411

San Remo Las Vegas
115 E. Tropicana Ave
• 702 739 9000

For more on casinos See pp36–7

On Levels 2-7
Near Elevators

Left **Wheelchair-access sign** Right **Monorail**

TOP 10 Las Vegas for Disabled Visitors

1 ADA Coordinators
Las Vegas is perhaps the world's most accessible city for people with disabilities. If you have any questions or any particular needs, have your travel agent contact the hotel's Americans with Disabilities Act (ADA) coordinator prior to your visit. Every major hotel-casino has one, responsible for ensuring that the facilities are accessible.

2 Airport Shuttles
Airport shuttles equipped with lifts are available at the airport baggage-claim area doors 1, 3, and 4. You may have to phone for a lift-equipped taxi, but direct-line phones are located in the baggage-claim area. Find out if car-rental company shuttles to their lots are lift-equipped, and let them know in advance if you need rear van seats removed and a ramp.

3 ADA Requirements
Bellagio, the Mirage, and Imperial Palace hotels have the reputation of being the best equipped for people with disabilities. All hotels, however, are supposed to have some rooms especially equipped for disabled guests. You may have to hunt around to find such specific amenities as roll-in showers, assisted-listening devices, vibrating alarm clocks, or televisions with telecaption devices.

4 Casino Accessibility
Every casino has accessible slot machines, and many have lowered tables with wheelchair access. Most bingo parlors have Braille and large-print game cards, and many casinos, if asked in advance, provide sign-language interpreters for gaming lessons.

5 Swimming Pools
Most hotels have lifts to assist guests into swimming pools; some of the pools with sand beaches also have wheelchair-accessible beach entrances.

6 Showroom Space
All Las Vegas venues for production and other shows (generally referred to as showrooms) have special areas for wheelchairs. Let personnel know in advance, since wheelchair users are often seated first.

7 Ramps and Restrooms
You can expect all public buildings, attractions, and hotel-casinos to be ramped and to have restrooms for the disabled. Curbs on most streets have been modified so that they are wheelchair accessible. City buses are fully accessible, as are some taxis, trams, shuttles, and the

monorail. It is also possible to rent motorized carts (mechanized one-passenger carts used in lieu of wheelchairs).

8 Medication Schedules
If you need to take medication at certain times, wear a watch – there are no clocks in casinos.

9 Pedestrian Overcrossings
Don't worry about having to climb stairs at overhead pedestrian crossings. They can be reached by elevators or escalators.

10 Information
ADA coordinators may be able to answer your queries. Try the website listed below, too.

Directory
www.vegasdisability info.com

Bellagio

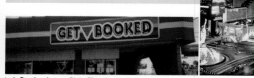

Left **Gay bookstore** Right **The city at night**

🔟 Gay and Lesbian Visitors

1 Acceptance
Opinions vary as to the degree of acceptance of gays and lesbians in Las Vegas. While the city is outwardly liberal and permissive – camp, even – its straight citizens are considered by some to be ultra-conservative in their views. Having said that, the city recently elected its first openly gay representative to the State Assembly. Many Las Vegas businesses, too, allow for what is euphemistically described as a "domestic partner" in their health-insurance plans.

2 Gay Organizations
There are more than 75 gay organizations active in Las Vegas, representing all sorts of interests, from singing to motorcycling.

3 Where the Action Is
The main gay section of Las Vegas, containing a number of gay bars and clubs, is in the Paradise Road, Harmon, and Tropicana avenues area, just east of the MGM Grand.

4 Clubs
If you feel at home with the younger crowd, head for Gipsy. Keys, meanwhile, offers sing-along piano-bar entertainment. Snick's Place has become something of an icon, being Las Vegas' oldest gay men's bar.

5 Transgender Bar
The Las Vegas Lounge is the city's only transgender bar.

6 Internet Information
You can get information about gay and lesbian venues in the city from several websites. Try www.gaynvegas.com for listings of accommodations and restaurants that are gay-owned or gay-friendly.

7 Meeting Venue
The Gay & Lesbian Community Center (known also just as The Center, *below*) sponsors frequent social events and is a venue for meetings of various gay and lesbian groups. It also offers free and confidential tests for HIV on Thursday afternoons from 3pm to 4pm.

8 Reading Material
Get Booked, the city's small but well-stocked gay bookstore, is open seven days a week.

9 Publications
For local gay-related news, pick up copies of the *Las Vegas Bugle* and *Out Las Vegas*. Both publications are available at local bars and at Get Booked bookstore.

10 Help Line
The organization PFLAG (Parents and Friends of Lesbians and Gays) runs a help-line, listed below.

Directory

Gipsy
4605 Paradise Road

Keys
1000 E. Sahara Ave

PFLAG Help Line
702 438 7838

Las Vegas Lounge
900 E. Karen Ave

Snick's Place
1402 S. Third Street

The Gay & Lesbian Community Center
912 E. Sahara Avenue
• 702 733 9800

Get Booked
4640 Paradise Rd
• Open 10am–midnight Mon–Thu, to 10am–2am Fri, noon–2am Sat, noon–midnight Sun

Websites
www.gayvegas.com
www.gaynvegas.com

Left **Bank of America sign** Center **ATM machine** Right **$100 bill**

TOP 10 Banking

1 Vegas Banking Hours

Most banks are open from 9am to either 5pm or 6pm Monday through Friday, and 9am–1pm on Saturday. Branches located in supermarkets tend to have longer hours and stay open all day on Saturday and on Sunday afternoon.

5 ATMs

Using ATM machines for cash and credit cards for purchases usually ensures the best exchange rates for foreign visitors. Be prepared to pay a small fee, which will be charged to your account, for using an ATM at a bank that is not your own. Instructions for use should appear in English and Spanish, and sometimes Japanese.

4 Drive-Through Banking

For many simple money transactions, drive-through banking (often spelled "drive-thru" on signs) is the most convenient method. The windows are usually open for an additional half-hour at the beginning and end of the bank's regular business day. Drive-throughs usually have cash machines (ATMs), too.

2 Getting Hold of Cash

Check-cashing services, located at various places along the Strip and downtown, charge large fees, so it's best to try to use alternative methods of getting cash. Cash advances on credit cards are available from cash-advance machines at all hotel-casinos, but again the service will cost you: the typical fee is 5 percent (that's a $50 fee for cashing $1,000), with larger percentages for smaller amounts.

3 Cashing Personal Checks at Hotels

Most hotels will cash guests' personal checks, provided they are in US dollars. It is not general policy, however, to cash checks for non-guests.

6 Foreign Currency

Unlike banks in Europe, only a few Las Vegas banks handle foreign currency. Most convenient of these is probably Bank of America. Many hotel-casinos will exchange foreign currency from major countries, but they charge a fee in addition to the hotel's own exchange rate.

7 Traveler's Checks

Traveler's checks can be cashed at any bank or hotel-casino. Try to get the checks in US dollars to avoid paying an exchange fee each time you cash one; if you do use checks in a foreign currency, try to get large denominations to save on fees when you cash the checks.

8 US Currency Denominations

US bank notes come in denominations as low as $1 and as high as $1,000.

9 Dollar Bills

If you are unfamiliar with US banknotes, take heed of the fact that they are notoriously hard to differentiate; pay special attention to this when handing over money to taxi drivers etc. A $1 "bill" is just the same size and color as a $20.

10 Small Change

The US dollar (sometimes referred to as a "buck") is divided into 100 cents (called pennies). Coins come in one cent, five cent (nickel), ten cent (dime), 25 cent (quarter), and 50 cent (half-dollar) denominations.

Directory

Bank of America
6900 W. Cliff Drive
• *702 654 6512*
• *Open 9am–5pm Mon –Thu, 9am–6pm Fri*

Left **Public Internet access** Center **Postage stamp** Right **Post Office sign**

TOP 10 Communications

1 Publications for Visitors

Useful entertainment guides include *What's On, Where, Today in Las Vegas, Vegas Visitor, Las Vegas Today*, and *Show Time*. Look out for the discount coupons for meals or shows.

2 Las Vegas Newspapers

The city's principal newspapers, the *Las Vegas Review-Journal* and the *Las Vegas Sun*, are both published daily, the former in the morning and the latter in the afternoon.

3 Internet Access

For the most inexpensive public Internet access, ask hotel personnel to direct you to the nearest

Public phone

eKiosk: there is a growing number of these facilities throughout the city. The typical charge is just $0.20 per minute, with a $2.00 minimum. Other Internet-access points are listed in the directory on this page; Kinkos is an outlet with several Las Vegas locations open 24 hours.

4 Making Calls

To place a call within Las Vegas and environs, omit the 702 area code. When telephoning outside the area, you will need to dial a 1, followed by the appropriate area code and seven-digit number. Local calls cost 35 cents for three minutes. The easiest way to pay for long-distance calls is to insert your credit card. As elsewhere in the world, calls made from hotel rooms cost a great deal more than those made from pay phones.

5 Public Telephones

You'll find public telephones, or pay phones, outside supermarkets and gas stations, and in restaurants, hotels, and casinos all around the area. When they're inside buildings, phones are usually located near the restrooms.

6 Cell Phones

If you want to rent a cell phone during your stay, consult the local yellow pages or have the hotel concierge obtain one for you.

7 Hotel Business Centers

Most major hotels have business centers for guests' use (although not for free) equipped with the latest computers; some also offer secretarial services and have guest rooms equipped with "dataports" for computers, fax, and internet usage.

8 Western Union

If you need to send international telegrams, ask hotel personnel where to find the nearest Western Union office. You can also use Western Union for wiring funds.

9 Post Offices

You can have incoming mail sent either direct to your hotel or to "General Delivery" at any US Post Office in the city. Two post offices that are conveniently located for visitors are the Downtown Station and the General Mail Facility.

10 TV and Radio

Choose from around 40 local radio and TV stations. If the local fare fails to satisfy, your hotel is very likely to have cable or satellite TV.

Directory

Cyber Stop Internet Café
3743 Las Vegas Blvd S.

Cyber City Café
3945 S. Maryland Parkway

Downtown Station
301 Stewart Ave
• Open 9am–5pm
Mon–Fri, 9am–1pm Sat

General Mail Facility
1001 E. Sunset Rd
• 6:30am–10pm
Mon–Fri, 8am–4pm Sat

For more sources of information See p115

Left **Security guard** Right **Parked car**

Things to Avoid

1 Traffic Tangle
Any street intersecting with Las Vegas Boulevard South means slow traffic, but drivers should avoid the Tropicana–Las Vegas Boulevard intersection altogether, if possible: it is the busiest intersection in the city and can take 15 minutes or more to get through.

2 Crime Zone
Although the Strip and the five-block Fremont Street Experience pedestrian mall are considered safe at any time, certain areas in North Las Vegas and on S. Maryland Parkway, around Sunrise Hospital, are not. The area north of Las Vegas library on Las Vegas Boulevard North is perhaps the roughest neighborhood in town. Do not walk there.

3 Con Artists
Rings of confidence tricksters – men and women – frequently operate in Nevada, with all sorts of scams. They prey primarily, but not exclusively, on the elderly. Beware anyone who approaches you with an offer that seems too good to be true, and never agree to collect jackpot winnings for another person on the promise that you'll be paid for doing so. Card sharps in particular look for suckers. Don't be one: if a deals sounds too good to be true, it probably is.

4 Resist the Girlie Clubs
Men are lured inside with bold promises, persuaded to pay extraordinary amounts for watered-down drinks, then sent on their way, not necessarily with the promised sexual favors. Prostitution is legal in the state of Nevada except in five counties, including Clark County. Las Vegas is in Clark County, so apprehended prostitutes and their customers are subject to fines and imprisonment.

5 Cache Your Cash
Don't wear expensive jewelry: it alerts robbers or pickpockets to the fact that you would be a lucrative target. Keep valuables in your room safe if there is one, or in the hotel's safe if there isn't. Keep your belongings with you at all times: the excitement of the bright lights, music, and carnival atmosphere can be distracting. If you win a large amount of money, ask for it in the form of a check rather than cash. Casinos will also provide security escorts for customers who request them.

6 Don't Let the Kids Roam
Do not allow youngsters under the age of 16 to go out on their own; children under 12 should not go without adults to malls or game arcades, even if they are in a group.

7 Car Trouble
Avoid poorly lighted garages and parking lots at night, especially when they seem deserted. Lock your car doors even when you are driving. Put all packages and luggage in the trunk. When you leave your car at valet parking, it's wise to remove anything of value and have only your car and trunk keys on the key-ring.

8 Mealtime Precautions
Cold soup and warm potato salad are potential sources of food poisoning, so when eating at buffets make sure that the food that is supposed to be hot is hot, and the food that is supposed to be cold is cold.

9 Panhandlers
It's up to you, of course, whether you give money to panhandlers (beggars), but you might consider contributing instead to charities that provide food and shelter for the homeless.

10 Law-Enforcement Officers
Despite the carefree atmosphere of Las Vegas, the police department is strict about enforcing the city's laws. Don't do anything here that you wouldn't do in your own home town.

For advice about traveling through the desert See p133

Left **Desert sign** Center **Temperature gauge** Right **Drugstore sign**

Ways to Stay Healthy

1 Becoming Acclimated

Give your body a chance to become acclimated upon arrival before engaging in strenuous activity, especially if you have traveled a long distance or from a much different climate or altitude. Because of the dry weather, for example, people prone to nosebleeds may experience problems.

2 Taking the Water

Nevada's low humidity means that you must drink plenty of fluids each day (alcoholic beverages don't count), especially during the summer. Dehydration and heat stroke account for many emergency medical service calls.

3 Solar Protection

Slather on the sunscreen whenever you go outdoors, not just when at the hotel pool. Even when the Nevada sunlight is filtered through clouds, it can burn.

4 Precautionary Measures

Pollution caused by blowing desert dust, vehicle emissions, and microscopic grit from construction sites can be a problem for people with respiratory problems.

5 Allergies and Arthritis

People with allergies to dust and sagebrush may have a problem in Las Vegas. However, most people with arthritis find that the low humidity is more comfortable for them than climates with higher humidity.

6 Overindulgence

Drinking too much is easy in the casinos' party atmosphere of bright lights and free drinks. It's up to you how much you indulge, but do not even think about driving afterward. Under Nevada law, the blood alcohol level at which a person is presumed intoxicated is 0.1 percent and can bring about a court appearance and heavy fine if the driver is stopped by police. In the case of an accident involving fatalities, it can result in imprisonment.

7 Insurance

Travel insurance may not be mandatory for visitors to the USA, but it is emphatically recommended because emergency medical and dental care can be extremely expensive. In most cases, people incurring medical expenses are required to make payment (or arrangement for it) before leaving the clinic, hospital, or physician's office.

8 Take Your Medicine

Remember that there are no clocks in casinos: the excitement of gaming may make you forget to take your regular medications. (Also be aware of those that shouldn't be taken with alcohol.) To have prescriptions filled, go either to drugstores (pharmacies) or the pharmacy departments of supermarkets, several of which are open 24 hours.

9 In Case of Illness

Since Las Vegas has more tourists than any other US destination, the medical professional is especially mindful of the need for in-room service (not usual in the USA). If you develop a condition that requires medical attention, Inn-House Doctor, Inc. offers free telephone consultations and the doctors make hotel visits if necessary. Nevada Resort Medical Services is a walk-in clinic that offers a free shuttle service and has doctors who make hotel calls. House Call Physicians specializes in in-room care for most types of medical problems.

10 Medical Emergencies

In case of an extreme medical emergency, dial 911 from any telephone (remember to dial the appropriate number to get an outside line if you're in your hotel room or dial "O" and ask the operator to dial it for you and send help to your room immediately.

Above **A desert walk just after sunrise, before ground temperatures rise**

🔟 Desert Precautions

1 Water Requirements
Be sure to carry drinking water. A gallon per person per day is suggested. The outdoor enthusiasts' greatest dangers are from hypothermia (extreme over-cooling) and heatstroke (extreme over-heating). Preventing dehydration helps avoid the latter. Carry water for your car, too. Even the radiators of new cars can overheat when outside temperatures hit 120°F (nearly 50°C).

2 Car Check
Be sure your car is in good mechanical condition and that it has a full gas tank. Stay on paved roads; do not drive on the shoulder, if possible, because there is danger of being trapped in the sand.

3 Flash Floods
Don't try to drive through flooded areas. If water begins to rise over the road, it is actually best to abandon your car and move to high ground.

4 Don't Go Solo
Never venture into the desert alone, and don't go hiking without a map and a good compass, even if you have a Global Positioning System (GPS).

5 Tell Somebody
Whenever you go hiking in the desert, advise a park ranger or other responsible person of your destination and estimated time of return. In case you become lost, search and rescue teams can work more effectively if they have information to guide them.

6 Dress Properly
Layered clothing slows dehydration and minimizes exposure. Summer temperatures up to 125°F (52°C). are not uncommon, and winter temperatures can plunge below freezing. During the course of a typical day and night, there may be a huge variation in temperature.

7 Be Prepared
Always carry a first-aid kit when hiking. Every hiker over the age of 12 should know CPR and basic first aid.

8 Dangerous Creatures
Beware of rattlesnakes and scorpions. Before you go, learn how to treat their bites (getting medical help as quickly as possible is recommended). Other dangerous animals and insects that live in the desert are gila monsters, mountain lions, wild boar, bears, killer bees, and centipedes. Wildlife may seem tame but will attack if they feel threatened or that their young are in danger.

9 Cover Your Head
Wear a hat to help prevent heatstroke whenever you are subjected to the desert sun's rays in the middle of the day – even when it is overcast. Even if you spend only minutes outside, you should protect your skin with sunscreen and use lip balm. Moisturizer is helpful in the desert climate as well.

10 Curb Your Curiousity
Stay away from abandoned mines. They are very dangerous because of the possibility of cave-ins, sharp drop-offs, and deadly gases.

Directory

Emergency Number
911

Inn-House Doctor, Inc
702 259 1616

Nevada Resort Medical Services
8th Flr, Suite 1, Imperial Palace • 702 893 6767

House-Call Physicians
1 800 DOCS 911

Left **Wigwam** Center **RV Parking lot entrance, Laughlin** Right **Tent in a national park**

TOP 10 Camping and Houseboating

1 Research your Campsites

Camping in city parks is generally not permitted. Camping in state and national parks is permitted in spaces designated for that use, and some off-trail overnight camping for hikers is allowed. Most state and national park and recreation area campgrounds have a first come, first served policy, so arrive early to have a better chance of getting a site. However, since other campgrounds require reservations, you'll need to contact them in advance. Be sure to obey all campground rules regarding fires, keeping pets on a leash, and the disposal of trash.

2 Tent Sites

There are only 15 tent sites at Red Rock Canyon but if you are lucky enough to find one free you can stay up to 14 days. There are also tent sites at Mt. Charleston and campsites around Lake Mead.

3 Reservations

Make reservations at privately owned campgrounds as far in advance as possible. As camping increases in popularity, it is more difficult to get a space without reservations. This is especially true during the summer when schoolchildren are on vacation and in the early autumn, a favorite holiday time for seniors.

4 Casino Campgrounds

It's especially important to reserve early if you want to stay at one of the casino camping facilities. Circusland RV Park is adjacent to Circus Circus on the Strip, and Sam's Town RV Park is near Sam's Town Hotel & Gambling Hall.

5 RV-Friendly Parking Lots

Laughlin is the most RV-friendly area in southern Nevada. Recreational vehicles can be parked in its casino parking lots overnight and there are several recreational vehicle parks on the other side of the Colorado River in Bullhead City, Arizona.

6 RV Rentals

If you would like to rent a recreational vehicle while you're in Las Vegas, you can choose from more than half a dozen rental companies. You will find them listed in the yellow pages of the Las Vegas telephone directory and on the Internet.

7 Campground Caution

Never camp in or near a dry wash (the course water takes when it rains) because of the potential for flash floods. Do not camp on the top of a large hill because of the danger from lightning and extreme winds.

8 Downpours

If you are camping in the desert when heavy rains begin, move to high ground immediately – at least 30 to 40 ft (10 m) above the canyon floor or bottom of a dry wash is recommended.

9 Houseboating

To rent a houseboat, contact either Seven Crown Resorts or Forever Resorts well in advance. The Forever Resorts marina at Callville Bay, the closer of the two, is about a 45-minute drive from the Las Vegas Strip.

10 Season Selection

Summer may be unpleasantly hot but is the peak season for campers and houseboaters: make arrangements up to a year in advance. The best rental values are during the winter, but the weather may not be pleasant. Consider renting a houseboat either during spring or fall.

Directory

Circusland RV Park
500 Circus Circus Drive
• 800 634 3450

Sam's Town RV Park
4040 S. Nellis Blvd •
702 454 8056

Seven Crown Resorts
800 752 9669

Forever Resorts
800 255 5561

Left **Mule riding** Center **Luxury hotel interior** right **New Year celebrations, the Strip**

🔟 Tips on Booking a Hotel

1 Choose an Appropriate Hotel
Take your personal travel style into consideration when choosing where to stay. If you like action and don't mind noise, you will want to stay on the Strip or downtown. If gaming will play only a minor part in your holiday, you will be better off staying at a hostelry that doesn't have a casino.

2 Travel Agents
The easiest way to reserve Las Vegas rooms is by having a travel agent book them for you. However, travel agents often do not have access to money-saving resources or time to access them.

3 Arrangements on the Internet
Almost all major Las Vegas hotel/casinos have their own Web sites on which they offer online bookings and advertise promotions. These are listed under their main entries within this book.

4 Packages
Explore the many airline/ accommodations packages. The least expensive of these are gambling junkets that usually include airline flights and two- to four-night hotel stays, based on double occupancy. There are often, but not always, several hotel choices in various price categories.

5 Individual Requirements
To make the most satisfactory room arrangements, phone the hotel directly to talk with a reservationist. By discussing your needs with a person who knows the hotel intimately, you have more assurance of getting that room with a certain view, on a lower (or higher) floor, or near the elevator, etc.

6 Bargains
For rock-bottom Las Vegas room rates, time your stay to coincide with the days preceding and following New Year's Eve and New Year's Day (or the entire weekend if New Year falls within one), as well as the days between the National Finals Rodeo and Christmas.

7 Times to Avoid
Room rates are usually higher over weekends and can more than quadruple when there is a major convention at the hotel or nearby (see p117).

8 National Parks
National parks in the USA have become extremely popular in recent years – especially those in the American southwest. The effect of this is that booking accommodations within the parks, as well as whitewater rafting and mule rides at Grand Canyon should be made at least a year in advance. Otherwise, you will have to stay in an outlying area.

9 Outlying Areas
Accommodations in Laughlin, Boulder City, Mesquite, and areas within the Las Vegas orbit are not as difficult to obtain nor as expensive as most of those in Las Vegas or Henderson.

10 Last-Minute Rates
If you are extremely flexible, you can take advantage of last-minute cancellations even when the city is at its most crowded by calling the Las Vegas Convention & Visitors Authority (see p115).

Houseboats in the Seven Crown Resort

Index

Page numbers in **bold** type refer to main entries.

Index

Acknowledgments

The Author
Connie Emerson, who has lived in
Nevada for more than 30 years,
writes travel articles for national
and international publications.

Produced by Blue Island Publishing,
Highbury, London

Editorial Director
Rosalyn Thiro

Art Director
Stephen Bere

Editors
Michael Ellis
Charlotte Rundall

Designers
Tony Foo
Ian Midson

Picture Research
Ellen Root

Research Assistance
Amaia Allende
Emma Wilson

Main Photographer
Demetrio Carrasco

Other Photographers
Tim Ridley
Alan Keohane

Artwork
Chris Orr & Associates

Proofreader
Stephanie Driver

Index
Hilary Bird

AT DORLING KINDERSLEY:

Director of Publishing
Gillian Allan

Senior Publishing Manager
Louise Bostock Lang

Publishing Manager
Kate Poole

Senior Art Editor
Marisa Renzullo

Cartography Co-ordinator
Casper Morris

DTP
Jason Little

Production
Sarah Dodd, Marie Ingledew

Cartography
Encompass Graphics

Dorling Kindersley would like to
thank all the hotels, restaurants,
shops, museums, galleries, and
other sights for their assistance
and kind permission to photograph
at their establishments.

Placement Key: t = top;
tl–top left; tr–top right;
c–center; cb–center below;
b–bottom; bl–bottom left;
br–bottom right; l–left;
d–detail.

Courtesy of THE BELLAGIO:
Russell MacMasters Photography
2tl, 14b, 15c, 31br, 46b, 50c, 77c,
120tl; BUREAU OF RECLAMATION:

Acknowledgments

Andrew Pernick 92t.

Courtesy of CAESARS PALACE: 74tl, 76tr; courtesy of THE CENTER: 128b; CIRQUE DU SOLEIL: photo Veronique Vial Costumes Dominique Lemieux 38c, 119c; © Al Seib 38b; CORBIS: Bettmann 30c, 31t, 120tr.

Courtesy THE DESERT INN: 135tc.

Courtesy of EFX: 38tr, 118tc, 119tc, 119tr; courtesy of EXCALIBUR: 135tr.

Courtesy of THE FORUM SHOPS: 26t, 26b.

Courtesy of GET BOOKED: 128tl.

Courtesy of HARRAH'S: 36tr; HULTON ARCHIVE: Archive Pictures 30tc.

Courtesy of JUBILEE: 3tcl, 39t.

Courtesy of LAS VEGAS HILTON: 56c; LAS VEGAS SUN: Lori Cain 58tr; Steve Marcus 58b; Aaron Mayes 85, 87tr; Sam Morris 59t, 86b; Ethan Miller 84tr, 87cb, 87bl; Marsh Starks 58tl, 59b; LORD OF THE DANCE: 38tc, 118tl.

Courtesy of MANDALAY BAY: 43t, 112tr; courtesy of the MGM GRAND: 42tl, 42b, 126b, 128tr; courtesy of THE MIRAGE 64tl, 64b, 66b, 73b, 117tr; courtesy of MONTE CARLO RESORT: 36b.

NHPA: David Middleton 104c.

STONE: Stewart Cohen 6t, 8–9; Kerrick James 110–11; Jake Rajs 6bl, 12, 80t.

Courtesy of STRATOSPHERE TOWER: 56tl, 56b.

Courtesy of TREASURE ISLAND: 76tl; courtesy of TROPICANA RESORT AND CASINO: 38tl.

Courtesy of THE VENETIAN: 20t, 32tl, 71t.

Jacket: All special photography, except CORBIS: Vittoriano Rastelli F/C ca; Hubert Stadler F/C cb; Karen Tweedy-Holmes F/C bottom.

All other images are © Dorling Kindersley. For further information see www.dkimages.com